DIGITAL DISTRESS

Growing Up Online

Lisa K. Strohman, JD, PhD
Melissa J. Westendorf, JD, PhD

WGAW Registration # 2010608

ISBN: 978-0-578-91685-9 (print)

Printed in the United States of America.

Dedication

This book is dedicated to all of the young people who have taken their lives due to technology-related issues, and to the parents, teachers, coaches, and concerned adults everywhere working to prevent such tragedies from ever happening to other families. Although we can never bring back the children we've lost, nor can we ever erase the pain from their families' hearts, we *can* learn from the past and work to prevent this from happening in the future.

Contents

Foreword

WHEN I BEGAN SPEAKING TO ADOLESCENTS AND YOUNG adults in the early 1980's about their interpersonal health and the looming threat of a condition we were just beginning to refer to as AIDS, I never imagined the risks that young people would be facing in our present age. I became aware of Dr. Strohman years ago and I have been relying on her to help me fully digest the risks of the digital world and screens. She has been an invaluable resource to help me tackle a world that I don't always fully grasp.

In this encyclopedic effort Dr. Strohman has partnered with her colleague Dr. Westendorf to create the ultimate source for helping parents navigate the confusing digital world. Drs. Strohman and Westendorf, because of their extensive clinical and forensic experience, know precisely what topics are important to address. Moreover their recommendations are informed by the latest evidenced based science and their years of experience working with young patients. It is no longer reasonable for parents to remain uninformed about the dangers of the digital landscape. It is exceedingly rare for a child not to be profoundly affected by the influence of digital media and thus necessary for parents to address this with the same diligence as any other threat to a child's health.

Just consider these numbers: Over 3 billion people use social media every month. 73% of American teens are on social media. 43% of kids have been bullied online; 1 in 4 have had it happen more than once. But did you know that only 1 in 10 children will inform a parent or trusted adult of their abuse?

So it is incumbent on the parent to understand the risk, how to detect it and how to respond. And this is significant not just for the well-being of our children but their mental health. Consider that bullying victims are 2-9 times more likely to consider suicide.

Bullying is just one of the many common issues that are reviewed by the authors. Pornography is another serious issue about which we as parents would rather ignore but we do so at our children's peril. We must educate ourselves to the facts. Porn is a $97 billion industry today, responsible for 35% of Internet downloads. Children are typically first exposed to online porn by age 8 and many develop a daily viewing habit by age 11. This is one of my greatest fears for the development of the young brain. Young people are being exposed to material that exceeds the upper limit of the developing brain's ability to regulate. The full effects of this upon a young person's development is not yet fully understood. The good news is that you can be informed and armed with information. You can take action.

Drs. Strohman and Westendorf provide us with solutions on how we must approach these dangerous realities. The authors will arm you with techniques and realistic goals to help you achieve what they call a Goldilocks Zone. Most research today shows that there's a happy medium between excessive use and social media isolation. They remind us that the digital lives of our children is something more important than we typically consider.

While adults will proudly say that they don't use social media because "I have a life," for today's children their lives often take place on social media. By getting the balance right, understanding the potential risks, and with careful monitoring and structuring of your children's relationship with digital media, your children can be protected from the deleterious effects that have unfortunately become so terribly common.

Our children's ability to build interpersonal relationships is at risk of breaking down. Poor emotional intelligence, social awkwardness, poor communication skills, and a lack of empathy are the consequences of technology overuse. This need not necessarily be the future for our children. Thank you to Drs. Strohman and Westendorf for providing us the resource with which to address these issues effectively and protect our children's health.

—Dr. Drew Pinksy, MD

Preface

"We shape our tools and thereafter our tools shape us."
—MARSHALL MCLUHAN

ONE OF THE FIRST LESSONS MANY OF US LEARNED AS CHILdren was to never get into a car with a stranger. The mere thought of one of our own getting into a car with an unknown adult has long provoked boundless, utter terror in the hearts of parents everywhere, invoking our deepest fears of kidnapping, abduction, or worse.

Yet, here in the 21st century, what do we do when we open up our smartphones and summon an Uber or a Lyft?

We get into a car with a stranger. And we pay for the privilege, too.

This is a time in which the basic assumptions that we make about the world—such as the wisdom of not getting into a car with a stranger—are being upended at an increasingly rapid pace.

Many historians today are saying that the changes wrought by the Information Revolution will be just as disruptive as the changes of the Industrial Revolution. During the 19th century, people all over the world left behind farms and small villages, crowding into large cities on a scale never before seen in history, where work was automated, mechanized, and standardized to meet the needs of a whole new class of heavy industry. New technologies of the day, from the assembly line to indoor plumbing and electricity, created an entirely new way of living that was dramatically different from anything the world had ever seen before. We sometimes forget, for example, that it was only 65 years from the time the Wright Brothers took flight in North Carolina to the time that Neil Armstrong set foot on the moon.

Today, every time you and your children open up a web browser, text with friends on cell phones, or order a movie on demand from your cable provider, you are interacting with people from all over the world, all of which is leaving behind a trail of digital breadcrumbs that can be used by any number of people for any number of reasons, from tracking terrorists to selling you vacations. It's a scary new world, full of all sorts of amazing opportunities and terrifying pitfalls that we're only now beginning to understand how to navigate.

Of course, if you're picking up this book, then you probably want to know how to get your kids to stop playing video games all day or get them unglued from their phone. That's coming.

This book is an outgrowth of our work not only as clinical psychologists and attorneys, but as parents. Like so many of you, we spend our weeknights running around, shuttling kids to various practices, hounding them to do their homework, and trying to get semi-nutritious meals in their stomachs, all the while following up with our own work projects. Weekends are spent cheering on the sidelines of athletic competitions, listening to music recitals, and wondering how other parents somehow make it all look so effortless. But, with our work in technology overuse, we are witnessing the painful, human cost for a generation of young who are growing up never having known a world without 21st-century technology.

Pew Research Center reports that at least 95% of American teens now have access to a smartphone, while 45% of those young people report being online "almost constantly." Not surprisingly, Rasmussen Reports surveys in 2018 and 2017 also found that most Americans believe that young people play too many video games and spend too much time in front of their devices.

If those behaviors were occurring in a vacuum, then that might not be much of a source of concern. But, as with the Industrial Revolution before, these changes are happening at such a fast pace that the world has yet to catch up with them. As psychologists, one of the greatest challenges we face is simply gathering sufficient quality data to make informed decisions—let alone public policy—because by the time we gather accurate data about a particular piece of technology, it's either become obsolete or completely transformed, and we're on to the next technological adventure—from Friendster to MySpace to Facebook to Instagram to TikTok and whatever comes next.

These challenges have a human face. Over the past decade, the suicide rate for girls aged 10-14 has increased by 200% (for boys the rate has "only" risen 50%), and is one of the leading causes of death in this age group. We believe this increase is integrally tied to online incidents and cyberbullying. Young people are first being exposed to online pornography by the age of 8, with some developing a daily addiction to such material by the age of 11. In 2017, several students had their admissions offers rescinded from Harvard because of online behavior, while University of Nebraska football coaches have publicly discussed how they review prospective recruits' social media accounts before deciding to pursue a player, and, of course, many professionals have been fired in recent years for comments made on private social media accounts. Most troubling of all, law enforcement officials are also now finding captured online video chats between pre-teens showing up on child pornography websites, without having the legal authority to stop their transmission around the world.

Given the magnitude of the problem, there simply isn't enough time in the day for either of us to see all of the concerned parents, troubled adolescents, or exasperated school administrators trying to solve this growing problem. What we hope to do with this book is offer every parent, grandparent, or caretaker some creative and practical solutions for the seemingly impossible task of balancing a healthy lifestyle with technology use.

—LKS / MJW
Phoenix, Arizona / Milwaukee, Wisconsin

Disclaimer: We Don't Hate Silicon Valley

The tech industry in America is one of the amazing success stories of our time and has made lives all across the world infinitely better. No one doubts the benefits of the life-changing medicine that has dramatically improved both the length and quality of our lives, nor the communications infrastructure that's enabled all of us to talk to each other around the globe instantaneously.

But every change brings with it both good and bad. While we don't aspire to turn back the clock to some romanticized version of the past, we *do* want to contribute our expertise to empower parents and families everywhere to build healthy lives that incorporate a *balanced* approach to technology. It is our hope that finding a balanced, sustainable relationship with technology will enrich all of our lives in the decades to come, while encouraging tech companies to develop future technology in a socially responsible way.

As the Chinese proverb says, "May you live in interesting times."

Who Should Read This Book

We are writing this book first and foremost because we are parents before we are professionals. Our own families have struggled with balance, boundaries, and the pain of allowing technology into our own homes. We have struggled with finding our kids awake at 2 am Facetiming with their friends on a school night and realizing we forgot to change the settings to limit our children's screen time. We assure you that our children have begged us repeatedly to have screen time and, at times, we have given in to the begging. We absolutely know that monitoring technology use is hard for everyone. Hence, we encourage everyone who works and cares for children to read this—not just parents but teachers, grandparents, daycare providers, coaches, counselors, Sunday school teachers, aunts and uncles, etc. We all have a stake in raising healthy, happy, and successful children—both our own and those around us.

Why *You* Should Read This Book

For so many of us, our children are the single greatest contribution we will make to the world, far above and beyond any accomplishments in the professional world. Parenting has always been a difficult endeavor, but today the task of raising up a contributing member of society is far more difficult—and different—than in previous generations.

While our children today don't face the same threats of disease and starvation faced in other times and places, they do face far more distractions along what's become an increasingly bumpy and complicated road to adulthood. Furthermore, as we'll show throughout the book, many of today's distractions are *designed* to be distracting. The days of a rambunctious young child like Dennis the Menace or Huckleberry Finn staring out the window during the school day have given way to young people glued to screens whose rich color schemes, loud noises, and design loops have all been engineered around a scientific understanding of human behavior.

The stories we illuminate in this book are based on both a reading of the most current literature in our field, a mosaic of clients we have treated, and cases we have discussed at various professional conferences. Any similarities to actual individuals are purely coincidental.

SIGNS OF THE 21ST CENTURY

- You haven't played solitaire with a real deck of cards in years.

- You have a list of 20 phone numbers to reach five people.

- You chat several times a day with a Nigerian prince over email, but you couldn't name your neighbor.

- When paying a cashier, you only know how to respond to "credit or debit"—what the heck is "cash?"

- You think "music in the air" refers to free downloads.

- You lose touch with any family member who doesn't have an email address.

- Second-day delivery takes way too long.

- You need PowerPoint to explain what you do for a living.

- A "half day" means leaving at 5 p.m.

- You find jokes on computers, not in books or word of mouth.

–Comedy Central

SECTION ONE
Background

CHAPTER ONE

Life in the 21st Century

"I tried to say, 'I'm a functional adult,' but my phone changed it to 'fictional adult,' and I feel like that's more accurate."
—READER'S DIGEST

I T'S A BRISK EARLY MORNING IN SUBURBAN AMERICA. OUTSIDE your window, the sun looms over the horizon and birds chirp cheerfully in the distance. The LCD display on your alarm clock turns to 6:00 a..m., jolting to life, and after an obligatory tap on the snooze button, you roll out of bed to face the day.

From the nightstand you pick up your smartphone, which has been charging overnight, and scroll through some social media before looking through team updates sent in from colleagues. A new batch of emails arrives, telling you what's in store for the workday.

As you and your family take turns in the bathroom with curling irons and cordless shavers, you flip on your favorite morning news program, where reporters file stories in real time from all over the world with satellite video phones. Meanwhile, in your utility closet, the water heater keeps everyone from *really* waking up with a cold shower.

Elsewhere in the house, the automatic coffee maker springs to life as your kids make their way to the kitchen for breakfast, devices in hand as they play along to the latest online craze that keeps them up at night while another group chat has them going back and forth with their friends. Somewhere amidst the chaos, for a moment, you find a bit of silence.

The traffic app on your phone says that your commute this morning shouldn't be too bad, but that you should avoid the construction on one of the local interstates. You drop the kids off at school, asking them if there's enough lunch money loaded on their student ID cards. Earbuds firmly in their ears, one blurts back, "It's fine," while the other asks, "Huh?"

Rolling your eyes, smiling, and shaking your head, you pull away, tuning in to a podcast or maybe some classic rock on your favorite satellite radio station. In the back of your mind, you're thinking about those work projects, a fight one of your kids might have had at school, which bills you need to pay online before you meet for lunch with a client, an Amazon Prime delivery scheduled to arrive that evening, and a show you've been wanting to stream on Netflix. Until you pass an accident on the roadway—someone texting and driving again—your first thought is that life is good, but busy. Merging in with traffic, you make your way down the road, open up your smartphone, insert your ear piece, and start through your list of calls to make before arriving at the office.

THE FIVE LIFESTYLE ATTRIBUTES THAT REALLY MATTER

IN ORDER OF PRIORITY

More money

Fewer hassles

More time

More choices

No worries

Source: *What Americans Really Want… Really* by Dr. Frank Luntz, Hyperion, 2009

Such is life in today's world. So much technology has become embedded in our daily lives that we lose perspective on how much it influences us—until the power goes out, the cable television doesn't work, we're snowed in at an airport, a bill goes unpaid, or our credit card is declined and we find out that our kids ordered 50,000 extra lives in the latest online game they're playing.

The first step in solving any problem is to acknowledge that there is one, and for that to happen we have to first understand the context of the problem, so let's start with the basics.

What Is Technology?

For the purposes of this book, we define technology as anything that can be turned on or off, including but certainly not limited to:

- Computers
- Gaming devices
- Cell phones
- Television sets
- Digital music players
- Tablets and handheld computers
- Children's interactive talking toys
- Blu-Ray, DVD, and other digital video players
- Digital recorders

So, is technology itself good or bad? In a word, yes. Technology is both good *and* bad, depending on how we use it. For example, when we give our children cell phones, *we* can contact them at any time, almost anywhere in the world. But we also lose control over *who else* can contact them, as was the case when our parents and grandparents had one land line, if not one telephone, at home. A solution to one problem creates a whole new set of problems, and in this case things are made all the worse when your children are light years ahead of you in knowing how to *use* the technology.

The world is changing rapidly, and with that change comes the good, the bad… and the ugly.

DIGITAL DISTRESS

TECHNOLOGY IN THE 21ST CENTURY... A SAMPLING

The Good	The Bad	The Ugly
Always connected	No boundaries between personal and professional life	Companies collect thousands of data points on every American consumer
Connect with distant relatives, childhood friends/classmates, and former work colleagues	Online connections are a poor substitute for face to face interaction	Loss of friendships over ideological differences introduced online
Interact with companies, celebrities, and elected officials like never before	Professional repercussions for every interaction online	Outside agitators sow social discord with hate speech and appeals to racism, sexism,nationalism, xenophobia,etc.
Ability to buy goods from allover the world	Loss of local retailers	Worldwide sale of illegal drugs across the dark web
Virtual reality simulation scan transport people anywhere in the world	Virtual reality pornography undercuts romantic relationships	Livestreams of young people captured and sold on child pornography websites

What Is Technology Overuse?

One of the biggest challenges in the emerging field of technology addiction is finding the right words to define exactly what is happening to our bodies when we interact with technology, and as you might expect, the exact wording of various concepts is subject to intense debate at professional conferences.

66% of parents feel their teens spend
too much time on mobile devices

52% of kids agree.

Source: "Technology Addiction: Concern, Controversy,
and Finding Balance", Common Sense Media, 2016

In the broader world we all joke about being "addicted" to a favorite TV show, a favorite video game, a particular kind of food, or a takeout restaurant down the street from our office. In the diagnostic sense, however, addiction has two main components:

1. Behavior that causes a problem—drug use, overeating, gambling, playing video games over and over, etc.

2. The continued practice of that behavior despite negative consequences.

Illegal drug use is bad for you, of course. That much we all know. But there's quite a difference between people who use illegal drugs *once* versus those who use illegal drugs *on a consistent basis* such that it harms them, bankrupts them, causes the loss of jobs, ends a romantic relationship, etc.

When working with children on technology issues in our clinics, we prefer the term "overuse" because "addiction" continues to be a loaded term that can be dangerous when applied to our children, particularly in an era of permanent, portable, medical records and the lifelong labels that they can place on a developing child. However, we recognize that the term addiction is a common term known to all and will use the two interchangeably throughout this book.

Among adults, an addiction is often thought of as a character flaw as much as a medical condition or neurochemical vulnerability. An adult battling alcoholism is typically expected to have to "hit rock bottom" to begin the process of recovery. Unfortunately, either rightly or wrongly, successful recovery is usually defined only by complete and total abstinence towards the offending substance or behavior, along with the lifelong stigma of "once an addict, always an addict."

These common beliefs provide the basis for an impractical approach to our children and their technology use. Our children are growing and developing in a world saturated with technology that requires us to adjust our beliefs and approaches accordingly. They haven't yet developed the critical judgment or maturity of an adult, so in much the same way that children are generally tried for crimes in a separate juvenile court system rather than alongside adults, we believe that it isn't realistic or appropriate to use adult addiction standards in the clinical evaluation of technology use in children.

Equally importantly, the placing of the label of "addict" on children specifically can create a dangerous self-fulfilling prophecy. Labeling a child as an addict means that he or she is likely to be viewed in certain ways by the adults responsible for his or her care in a way that can create a vicious, downward spiral that affects the child's future prospects. Conversely, a child who is labeled as gifted may often be given the benefit of the doubt or have behaviors explained away in ways that he or she does not deserve.

In light of the above, we define technology "overuse" to be when a child feels the need to use a piece of technology and finds separation from that technology to be extremely overwhelming, resulting in rage, anxiety, depression, or manipulative behavior in an effort to reconnect with it. For example, as part of our presentations to parents and schools, we often show videos of children breaking down crying when parents won't let them use their iPads, along with kids trying to break down doors to the family computer room when it's time for dinner. If you're an adult who's left home without your cell phone and felt naked without it, then you understand how your children are feeling. You just hide it better!

Of course, like any new concept, technology addiction is not without its critics and they deserve some attention.

So, Is Technology Overuse Really A Thing?

"It's not a drug, but it might as well be.
It works the same way… it has the same results."
—DR. ROBERT LUSTIG, professor of pediatric endocrinology
at the University of California, San Francisco as quoted at a
conference of the Center for Humane Technology in 2018

Yes, most definitely. As we'll expand upon in chapter 4, "process addictions" can function within the brain in much the same way as actual chemical addictions. The most well-known process addition today is gambling, and most responsible adults today understand the possible addictiveness of that behavior and accord gambling the respect it deserves. Although we can all enjoy a trip to Las Vegas or Atlantic City from time to time, or a weekly game of cards with friends, anyone who's ever visited those gambling meccas has seen the toll taken on adults who lose every penny they own at a blackjack table or who spend days upon days feeding one coin after another into a slot machine. While that certainly doesn't happen to *everyone* who enjoys a stay at Las Vegas or Atlantic City, it happens often enough to warrant genuine public concern, as well as pushback against the companies making billions in profit along the way.

The scientific consensus on technology addiction today is building. In 2013, the American Psychiatric Association, in the most recent update of its Bible for the mental health field, the *Diagnostic and Statistical Manual of Mental Disorders* (the "DSM" or "DSM-5" in its fifth edition), placed what is being called "Internet Gaming Disorder" under a section entitled "Conditions for Further Study," in the hopes of encouraging additional clinical research. In 2016, the American Academy of Pediatrics released its first set of guidelines for media use among children and adolescents and developed some early best practices for how parents and pediatricians can find an appropriate, balanced approach to media use. Most recently, the World Health Organization is now including in its 2018 edition of the "International Classification of Diseases" (the "ICD") language about Internet Gaming Disorder as well.

Taken together, this emerging critical mass means that the medical profession now can no longer ignore the role that technology plays in our lives as well as its effect on all of us. Naturally, this rise in concern has generated a backlash from critics, so let's address them now.

Common Arguments Against Technology as a Platform for Addiction

Critics of technology addiction as a field describe the rise in concern in recent years as a possible "moral panic" no different from the Salem Witch Trials of colonial America or the belief among some in recent decades that rock 'n roll songs played backwards contained Satanic chants. We beg to disagree. We believe this is a genuine problem with real life consequences, so let's go ahead and address some of the common arguments made against technology addiction, one by one:

ARGUMENT #1: Technology is not a drug

Technology itself is not a drug in the traditional sense. However, what matters here is not the introduction of a foreign substance into the body but how repeated, compulsive behaviors can have the same effect on the body as if those behaviors were a drug. The upfront actor may be different, but the end result is the same. This is a process addiction, much like a gambling or sexual addiction.

ARGUMENT #2: Technology addiction is not common

PERCENTAGE OF AMERICAN TEENS WHO HAVE ACCESS TO:

88% Desktop/laptop computer

95% Smartphone

PERCENTAGE OF TEENS WHO SAY THEY USE THE INTERNET
2018:

45% Almost Constantly   44% Several Times a Day

2014-2015:

24% Almost Constantly   56% Several Times a Day

Source: Pew Research Center, "Teens, Social Media & Technology 2018"

The common sense experience of any parent today tells us that this is false, both in raising their own children and in working with young people entering the workforce who seem incapable of putting their phones down. Your intuitions are backed by a growing body of research, and although, as with gamblers in Las Vegas or Atlantic City, only a certain percentage of kids will go on to have problems that rise to the level of true addiction to technology, it's an issue that we as parents must manage from an early age before it becomes a problem. *This is a choice,* and something we *all* have to deal with today, one temper tantrum at a time.

ARGUMENT #3: Technology addiction is not a mental illness

This again is an issue of semantics. While technology addiction may not be officially considered a "mental illness" at present, at a minimum we can all consider it a treatable condition.

The debate over technology addiction today has less to do with how your children interact with phones, computers, iPads, etc. and more to do with the back end operations of medicine—whether health professionals can enter diagnostic codes into computers so that patients can receive treatments, doctors can administer care, and insurance companies will pay for those treatments. The debate over terminology, diagnostic criteria, etc. is ultimately about building a common understanding of the issue so we can generate proper care based upon rigorous science, and with billions of dollars at stake, you can bet that the tech industry is going to weigh in as well.

ARGUMENT #4: Technology addiction is not caused by technology

This argument is only partly true. Overuse of technology and the overstimulation of the brain from technology impacts the brain *like a drug*. Drugs themselves like cocaine and marijuana are not as much the issue as it is *how they affect the brain*. What makes cocaine and marijuana dangerous to the body (rather than, say, a glass of orange juice) is the damage that they do to the body and how they affect our ability to live our lives. Today, we have a much deeper understanding of how the brain works and can understand how our interactions with the outside world can, over time, change the actual structure of our brains. For example, although a casino chip or a deck of cards isn't addictive by itself, the act of gambling and the neurochemical rush it provides some people can become addictive, and cause the same problems as traditional addictions.

Secondly, although a particular piece of technology like a cell phone may not itself be addictive, many of the apps designed for those platforms *are* addictive, and are designed to be as such. It is not an accident, for example, that many cell phone apps use certain color schemes and provide their users with certain "rewards" in ways that hijack the body's hardwired responses to stimulus, just as so many casinos have bright lights and bells and whistles everywhere. The resorts in Las Vegas and Atlantic City were not built by "the house" losing.

ARGUMENT #5: Technology is not uniquely addictive

What is important to understand here—and where tech companies have a legitimate point of disagreement—is that *anything* can become addictive. Anything that makes us happy and causes us to repeat a behavior can become an addiction.

Parents today need to understand that tech companies are now hiring behaviorists with PhDs in psychology to work alongside designers and pro-grammers to specifically design their products to be as addictive as possible. Companies are making their money—sometimes billions of dollars—based upon how long users engage with their products, and thus the companies are engineering an understanding of how humans naturally respond to stimuli right into their products. The belief among some in the tech industry is that if they merely design their products to be useful—rather than addictive—they won't be able to generate profits, let alone recoup venture capital investments. Meanwhile, someone somewhere else will simply design a better (i.e. more addictive) mousetrap, and make those billions in profit instead.

What also matters here is the genetic baggage that we each bring to our interactions with a piece of technology. Some young people have experienced seizures when playing loud, colorful video games, and that isn't necessar-ily the fault of the video game, or the intention of the game's designers—it's simply the collision of the child's genetic vulnerabilities with just the right stimulus to create that perfect storm. Knowing that, we as parents have to ensure that our children are protected from these dangers by understanding both the unique biology of our individual children and the possible dangers they face when interacting with different pieces of technology, along with just how addictive some devices, apps, and online content truly can be.

ARGUMENT #6: Technology, itself, does not lead to suicide

Pieces of technology themselves are not linked to either depression or suicide, although the overuse of technology and the apps available on them have been linked to depression. The question here is one of the chicken and the egg—whether the technology or the depression comes first.

That said, the *interactions* we can have on a piece of technology *can* lead to depression and suicide. In our private practices, we've worked with children who have attempted suicide due to naked pictures being sent around entire schools, the loss of a girlfriend, or chronic bullying. In these cases, the combination of adults not understanding the extent of their children's interactions online, combined with children making their usual youthful mistakes, creates a toxic environment in which some children have been led to the brink of suicide, while others go on to take that fatal, final step. Although tech companies do deserve a portion of the blame for how their products are designed and marketed, we as parents still have that responsibility to do our homework on the technology our children are using and to ensure that their interactions are responsible and developmentally appropriate, lest they become part of that painful spike in suicides mentioned at the beginning of the book.

Of course, we don't want to give the impression that all technology is bad all the time, or that buying your kid an iPhone for their birthday will automatically lead to a vicious cycle of depression and suicide. These issues can happen to anyone, and many of the parents we work with find themselves saying that they never imagined that this sort of thing would happen to them, or that they never imagined that their child would act in a certain way. That's a matter of being informed, and finding what we call the "Goldilocks Zone."

The Goldilocks Zone

Somewhere between the extremes of 24/7 connectedness and living off of the power grid in rural Alaska, there's a balance that scientists often refer to as the "Goldilocks Zone." In the childhood fairy tale of Goldilocks and the Three Bears, a young girl wanders into a home belonging to three bears and comes upon three bowls of porridge. One bowl is too hot, one bowl is too cold, and one bowl is juuuust right. Finding that balance—the Goldilocks Zone—is what this book is about.

Right now, several European countries are pushing back against American and Asian tech companies, trying to find that balance. For example, several European countries have debated the "Right to be Forgotten," meaning that we ought to have the right to delete ourselves from Internet searches, along with a "Right to Disconnect," meaning that employees legally ought not be required to answer work emails after a certain hour, and a "Right to Repair," meaning that tech devices should be able to be fixed by the general public rather than discarded at the slightest problem or only serviced in expensive boutique stores.

As we'll discuss later, many concerned parents like you are not only reading up on technology addiction but creating tech-free nights at home to push back against the saturation of technology in our lives. Not surprisingly, some families are reporting to us that some of their happiest, most memorable times together have been on nights when the power went out and they were forced to play a board game together by candlelight.

Finding that balance is always a challenge, but such is life in the 21st century. As many authors have noted, we are more connected than ever before, and yet that isn't always a good thing. So now let's take a look at how today's children are growing up in a unique environment, and how that separates them from previous generations.

KEY TAKEAWAYS FROM THIS CHAPTER

- The world has dramatically changed, even in our lifetimes, and the pace of change is expected to continue to accelerate.

- Technology addiction is one of the growing issues of our time, backed by a growing body of research, making the task of finding the balance between technology and humanity one of the ongoing challenges of our time.

- Among children, the term "overuse" is preferable over "addiction" to avoid the stigma associated with adult classification.

- Technology can affect our children in profound ways and their only hope is an educated parent who makes informed decisions about technology use in their household.

FOR FURTHER READING

- *Glow Kids: How Screen Addiction is Hijacking Our Kids–and How to Break the Trance* by Nicholas Kardaras

- *Alone Together: Why We Expect More from Technology and Less from Each Other* by Sherry Turkle

- *What Americans Really Want… Really* by Dr. Frank Luntz

- *The Next Hundred Million: America in 2050* by Joel Kotkin

- *The Rise of the Creative Class* by Richard Florida

CHAPTER TWO

Introducing Generation Z

"I realized my little nephew will never know life without Facebook.
He'll never know what it's like to go,
'I wonder what happened to that guy Chris from high school?'
and then just shrug his shoulders and move on."
—OPHIRA EISENBERG

EVERY FALL, BELOIT COLLEGE IN WISCONSIN PUBLISHES A "Mindset List" to distill for its faculty and staff the worldview of the incoming students that will soon be populating their campus.

The Mindset List is an excellent example of the small, continual creep of generational change. For example, the shared experiences for students in the graduating class of 2022, entering in the fall of 2018, include:

- Outer space has never been without human habitation.
- They have always been able to refer to Wikipedia.
- They have grown up afraid that a shooting could happen at their school, too.
- Investigative specials examining the O.J. Simpson case have been on TV annually since their birth.

- Presidential candidates winning the popular vote and then losing the election are not unusual.
- They've grown up with stories about where their grandparents were on 11/22/63 and where their parents were on 9/11.
- The Prius has always been on the road in the U.S.
- A visit to a bank has been a rare event.
- The folks may have used a Zipcar to get them to the delivery room on time.
- Films have always been distributed on the Internet.

(Source: "The Mindset List: Class of 2022" by Tom McBride, Ron Nief, and Charles Westerberg, www.themindsetlist.com)

The generation gap between parents and children is one of the keys to understanding the differences between parents and children at all stages of life. Most of you reading this are parents of grade school to high school kids, typically in the middle of your career, and although your children are just getting started and you are in your prime, it's important to appreciate that the world was a very different place *when we were the same age* as our children are now.

Your 10-year-old child growing up in the American suburbs today experiences the world—and develops very different assumptions about the world—than a 10-year-old child growing up in other times and places. Although many things about being 10 years old never change, children today don't grow up fearing polio or a nuclear war between the U.S. and Soviet Union. Just the same, we typically haven't grown up with the fears that our children have today that terrorists would fly planes into buildings, that an armed shooter would enter the halls of our school, or that a global pandemic would alter the learning environment.

Even though our underlying biology stays the same, social norms change, the economy changes, the culture changes, and the demographics of the country change, all creating an endlessly evolving stew of influences that make each generation distinct from that which come before and that which comes after. This is why even within the same family, we all experience the same events in a slightly different way—because even though we may share the same biology, our realities are shaped by a different mix of experiences.

CHANGING FAMILIES

Percentage of children living with:

	1960	1980	2014
Two parents in first marriage	73%	61%	46%
Two parents in remarriage	14%	16%	15%
Cohabiting parents	-	-	7%
Single parent	9%	19%	26%
No parent	4%	4%	5%

Source: "Parenting in America," Pew Research Center, 2015

So, how exactly are kids different today, and how should that affect our parenting?

Who Is Generation Z?

Social scientists today generally consider the dividing line between the Millennial generation and Generation Z to be the birth years of the late 1990s to the early 2000s. This sort of thing is generally more an art than a science though, and often best left to historians with the benefit of hindsight. There is little consensus right now, for example, on what constitutes the latter end of Generation Z, although we consider it to be somewhere around 2015. That said, several events mark a clear delineation between the children who grew up before them, and the children who grew up after them. This is a surprise to no one who lived through them—the explosion of the Internet, the shootings at Columbine High School, and 9/11.

PARENTS' HOPES FOR THEIR KIDS

Percent saying this trait is extremely important to them

71% Honest and ethical

65% Caring and compassionate

62% Hardworking

54% Financially independent

45% Ambitious

Source: "Parenting in America," Pew Research Center, 2015

The children who have grown up this century in the aftermath of certain events see the world very differently than the Millennials who came of age before them during the 1980s and 1990s. Besides technology, several traits distinguish Generation Z from the Millennials:

The World has Never Felt Safe

The children who have grown up after 9/11, following the passage of the Patriot Act and the wars in Iraq and Afghanistan, know that terrorism isn't just something that happens to the rest of the world but that also happens on the homefront. Even worse, mass shootings and school shootings now seem routine, while the Great Recession, bank bailouts, corporate scandals, and the struggles of the middle class have all made them far more economically insecure than prior generations.

They're Accepting

Generation Z will likely be the last majority-white generation in American history, while states like California, Texas, Hawaii and New Mexico already have populations that are composed of a majority of ethnic minorities. Your children are the first generation to grow up with an African American president and two African American secretaries of state, as well as Latino and Asian governors and mayors of major cities, and the first female presidential nominee from a major political party. Gay rights has been the defining civil rights struggle of their lifetimes, and the diversity at home and connections to the rest of the world make them that much more accepting of differences between people than those who came before them.

They're Health Conscious

Today's children are the beneficiaries of the public health campaigns of recent decades and thus are less likely to smoke cigarettes, drink alcohol, consume illegal drugs, or get pregnant—and are much more aware of the nuances of nutritious food—avoiding fats, sugar, and fast food, while searching out for healthy, organic, sustainable options. For example, one survey of Generation Z's favorite restaurants found that McDonald's didn't even make the top five; top food destinations for today's young people include Starbucks, Chipotle, Chick-Fil-A, Panera Bread, and Olive Garden. Meanwhile, vaping is the new public health challenge now, along with changing opinions about marijuana.

They Value Their Privacy

Your children are also learning from the mistakes of their parents and older siblings in the digital space as well. As British journalist Rhiannon McGregor noted, "They're aware from an early age of how they're portrayed online and offline, so they curate themselves in a more conservative way." Although being a rebellious youth can be fun, with time they're becoming painfully aware of the consequences of reckless online behavior. Not surprisingly, the newer forms of social media that have been adopted by this generation (Snapchat, for example) are popular due to their "temporary" features, including disappearing texts or images, compared to the more permanent, etched in stone forever model of Friendster, MySpace, Facebook, Twitter, and LinkedIn that have preceded them. In addition, there are vault apps available to house personal images and data and virtual private networks (VPN's) to protect browsing histories.

They're Entrepreneurial and Worried about Their Future Prospects

With the 50-year careers, gold watches, and pensions of IBM and General Motors firmly in the rear view mirror, today's kids are growing up in the "Gig Economy" where they work independently for multiple companies, cobbling together a full-time job. They're learning the importance of hustle both online and in person, and struggling to build careers in an ever-evolving world.

They're Changing the Distinction between Adulthood and Childhood

Today's young people are much closer to their parents than previous generations and, despite being exposed to more and at a younger age, are much slower to leave the nest, to the disdain of parents, college administrators, and employers. The combination of higher college costs, the growth of unpaid internships, and competition also means that it's more difficult for them to establish themselves as adults than previous generations, pushing back both their abilities—and desire—to marry, have children, and buy a house. (Source: 7 Unique Characteristics of Generation Z, courtesy Oxford Summer School and Oxford Royale Academy)

Of course, many of the above differences have one common thread and the reason why you bought this book—technology.

Digital Natives vs Digital Immigrants

"It's not an addiction; it's an extension of themselves.
Are you addicted to your right hand?"
—FROM A PROFILE OF GENERATION Z

Most important to the unique story of Generation Z, of course, is technology, and perhaps the best metaphor we've heard thus far to explain the dramatic technological change in society over the last few generations is one so central to our identity as Americans: immigration.

Our children today are "digital natives," the native-born children of our generation of "digital immigrants," who possess the sort of intuitive, granular, and nuanced understanding of the technological landscape that we as "immigrants" will never fully understand, no matter how hard we try. The mere fact that we haven't grown up with the newer generations of technology that our children have means that, like an immigrant speaking a second language, we will always have an "accent" and commit the kind of subtle blunders that mark us as outsiders, while our children speak a language that we will only ever understand in superficial terms, and whose peculiarities are completely foreign to us.

Percentage of Households With Computer and Internet Use: 1984 to 2016

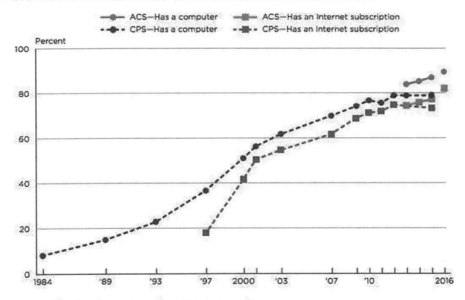

Note: For more information, visit <www.census.gov/cps> and <www.census.gov/acs>.
Source: U.S. Census Bureau, 1984-2015 Current Population Survey, 2013-2016 American Community Survey, 1-Year Estimates.

6 TERMS THAT SUMMARIZE GENERATION Z'S MINDSET

DIY: Do it Yourself. Think outside of the box to find solutions.

GPA: Grade Point Average. Pressure to get good grades and get into a good college.

FYI: For Your Information. Passing information back and forth between each other.

FOMO / FOLO: Fear of Missing Out / Fear of Living Offline. Seeing other people's lives online, more socially aware and less self-aware than before.

OJT: On the Job Training. Learn as you go.

OMG: Oh My God! Hyperbole, nonsensical humor, impulsive remarks online.

Source: Psychology Today, September 28, 2017

This immigrant-like experience of growing up in one time and place only to live in another time and place means that the new world in which we live will always be somewhat foreign and that our life's journey will be marked by a series of firsts that our children will never understand—the first time we used the Internet, the first time we bought a pager, our first cell phone, our first smartphone, downloading music for the first time, and shopping online for the first time, among others—along with an understanding of how each of those inventions has changed the world over time—the closure of daily newspapers, the closure of suburban shopping malls, and the removal of land telephone lines, for example. Meanwhile, to our children, these "firsts" will seem as foreign as when our own parents would have told us about bringing home a television set for the first time, buying a family car for the first time, or gathering around the radio during the Great Depression. Those were all monumental events in the lives of our parents and grandparents, and yet we often have trouble imagining the world without them.

The explosion of the Internet, the Columbine shootings, and 9/11 may have marked the line between the Millennial generation and Generation Z, but two more recent fault lines have also marked changes in society this century: 2007 marked the release of the iPhone, while 2012 marked the year in which a majority of Americans owned a smartphone. As of the writing of this book, for example, you would be as much of an outlier as an American adult if you *didn't* have a smartphone as if you were an American adult in the 1950s who *didn't* smoke cigarettes.

Neverending Adolescence

One of the most unexpected and frustrating challenges facing parents today is the issue of our children's maturity. Although adolescence might have been defined in previous generations as specifically the teenage years, the literature today is expanding the definition downwards to the age of 10, and upwards to the age of 24. By some reports, young people are not achieving full financial independence until the age of 35. And yes, we're about as thrilled to hear that as you are.

On the biological front, this is due primarily to the earlier onset of puberty in kids today, with some girls having their first period even while still in grade school. But on the social and emotional end, young people are experiencing all sorts of delays in taking on the roles and responsibilities that have traditionally marked the transition to adulthood—finishing school, adult employment, marriage, child rearing, and the purchase of home. For example, although adulthood has traditionally been defined by the age of 18 in most western countries, and still younger in some religious traditions, the Affordable Care Act has allowed young people to stay on their parents' health insurance plans up through the age of 26.

COMMON CONCERNS OF PARENTS

Percent worried that these may happen to their children

60% Be bullied

54% Struggle with anxiety or depression

50% Be kidnapped

45% Get beat up or attacked

43% Get pregnant / get a girl pregnant as a teenager

41% Have problems with drugs and alcohol

31% Get shot

27% Get in trouble with the law

Source: "Parenting in America," Pew Research Center, 2015

This has many implications for parents. Children today are less likely than teenagers in previous generations *at the same age* to have a driver's license, to work at a paid after school job, and to go out on dates. This puts us parents on the hook for much longer periods of time in driving our kids around from one activity to another, in giving them an allowance, and for covering expenses like a cell phone bill or extra money for new clothes. Our kids today also have a much larger window in time in which they're exposed to the risks of adolescence, like drug and alcohol addictions, school failure, unplanned pregnancies, and sexually transmitted diseases. And, far more so than in previous generations, today's parents find themselves supporting their adult children farther into adulthood than ever before.

Gender Differences

Although it's fashionable today in some circles to pretend that there are no differences between the two sexes, any parent with young children, and certainly any teacher or daycare worker will notice right away that yes, boys and girls are different. How much of that is innate (nature) and how much is how we are socialized (nurture) is of course the subject of endless debate, and provides endless fodder for standup comedians and romantic comedies.

Gender differences in the use of technology are not anything new; for example, different genders will often use the same *technology* but for very different *reasons*. Among adults, for example, men have traditionally used the Internet as a form of leisure while women are much more likely to use it to find information. Also among adults, men are much more likely to use social media to find new friends and professional contacts, while women are more likely to use social media to maintain their existing relationships with family and friends.

With our Generation Z children, boys are more likely to play video games (and potentially become addicted to them) while girls are more likely to use social media (and potentially become addicted to that). Interestingly, among younger children, rates of technology use are roughly equivalent among boys and girls, after taking into account the time boys spend on video games. Boys today are also spending more time developing their friendship networks through online video games (and less in real life, unfortunately) while girls tend to utilize social media platforms more often for much of the same reason.

Parents and teachers are also demonstrating gender biases in how they treat boys and girls in their use of technology. For example, although research has shown that boys and girls both enjoy taking computer courses for similar reasons, boys are more likely to enroll in those classes, and to behave more confidently and proactively in those classes, while girls tend to be more passive learners. And although research indicates parents are more likely to buy technology for sons than they are for daughters, they are likely to impose technology usage *rules* on their daughters than on their sons. This is where we as parents have to be careful of our unconscious biases in how we parent our children, and take advantage of the diversity efforts that are underway in the STEM fields. As we'll discuss in later chapters, this is also where we can be proactive in finding our children mentors and outside activities to circumvent whatever our children are—or are not—being exposed to in school, so our children can begin to advocate for themselves in academic and professional settings.

KEY TAKEAWAYS FROM THIS CHAPTER

- Generation gaps will always exist between parents and children no matter the age, because even with the same gene pool, the fact that we grow up in different times and places means that we are shaped by a different mix of forces than either our children or our parents, and sometimes even our own siblings.

- Today's children—those born after the Internet explosion, Columbine, and 9/11—are growing up in a much more insecure yet diverse and integrated world. They expect to be catered to commercially but are protective of their privacy, having seen the mistakes of older generations.

- Your children are also growing up more slowly and more differently. Although biological puberty now has its onset much earlier than in previous generations, children are taking much longer to grow up in terms of finishing school, building careers, and starting families.

- Today's children, having grown up in much more insecure times, are much more focused on pragmatic careers that yield tangible results, with their primary concern in seeking jobs to be salary and other compensation.

- Boys and girls today both use technology at high rates, but they often use different technology for different reasons.

FOR FURTHER READING

- *iGen* by Jean Twenge
- *Generations* by William Strauss and Neil Howe

CHAPTER THREE

The Developing Brain

"The brain is entirely fat... without a brain, you might look good, but all you could do is run for public office."
—GEORGE BERNARD SHAW

THE HUMAN BRAIN IS ONE OF THE MOST AMAZING structures anywhere in the known universe, and with all that science has uncovered in recent centuries, that isn't something to be said lightly. Only a few species have had larger brains than our own *Homo sapiens*, yet none has ever had such a large brain relative to its body size. By comparison, for example, the human brain is *three times* the size of our nearest biological cousin, the chimpanzee. That cognitive advantage is what has, over time, allowed our species to not only write symphonies and explore distant planets, but to shape the natural world to serve our needs.

Yet, as we all know, the human brain is not without its own blind spots and shortcomings, to say nothing of how we all use (or don't use) our brains, which keeps psychologists like us in business. Strokes, aneurysms, memory lapses, poor decisions, and even the occasional "senior moment" all reflect how the computing power that sits between our ears is still just as human as the rest of us. The last few decades of scientific research have yielded a gold mine as to how the brain works—and doesn't work—and the application of that understanding helps explain to a good degree why companies today are making so much money off of your children (off of all of us) looking at screens all day long. Even then, it's a testament to how much science has uncovered about the brain that we've begun to appreciate how little we know about this organ so central to our existence.

In this chapter we'll take a look at how your child's brain develops, from birth to adulthood, and then in the next chapter we'll examine how technology throws a wrench into this developmental process. As you'll see, more often than not, there is a biological basis for why your kids behave the way that they do.

Birth to Toddler Years: "Like A Blender Without a Lid"

"A 3 year old is basically a walking, talking middle finger."
—AMY DILLON

Like other mammals, human beings are born immature. And no, that's not meant as an insult to our children—we'll get to teenage issues later—it's a fact of nature. A newborn calf, for example, is able to walk on its own and fend for itself at a much earlier age than our own children, who take several months to learn how to crawl and then walk. Likewise, although we don't consider humans to be adults until the age of 18, and the brain isn't fully developed until the mid 20s, a typical monkey will develop its adult-sized brain by the age of 6 months. Humans are unique in that much of their neurological development takes place *after* they are born.

Your child arrives into the world with a brain comprised of around 100 billion neurons and an even more incomprehensible 100 trillion different connections ("synapses") between neurons in the cerebral cortex alone. In the first few years of life, your child's brain will build more than one million new connections between brain cells *every single second*.

This rapid burst of development only occurs twice in a life, the first being during the toddler years. It is also when the process of "pruning" begins to take place. Pruning is essentially how the brain becomes its most efficient self when the connections that aren't being used are allowed to wither away (in the same way that we would prune off the weak branches of a vine or tree), leaving more energy and focus for the connections that *are* being used. For example, when our children learn how to wave hello or goodbye, that action alone entails an incredibly complex set of brain-directed motor skills which are practiced over and over, reinforcing the successful movements and pruning away those that are not. Things are obviously a bit more complicated on the cellular level, but that's approximately how it works.

WHAT EVERY CHILD NEEDS TO PROMOTE BRAIN DEVELOPMENT

Interaction: consistent, long-term attention from caring adults

Touch: Holding and cuddling children helps their brain grow

Stable Relationships: Relationships with parents and other caregivers

Safe, Healthy Environments: Free of lead, loud noises, sharp objects, and other dangers

Self-Esteem: Respect, encouragement, and positive role models

Quality Care: Care from trained professionals when you can't be there

Play: Helps children explore their senses and discover how the world works

Communication: Talking with your children builds their verbal skills

Music: Teaches them new skills and offers a fun way to interact with them

Reading: Helps grow a healthy brain and create a lifetime love of books

Source: Family Development Resources, Inc. / NurturingParenting.com

Grade School: "iPhone, iPod, iPad ... iPaid!!!"

"Some children threaten to run away from home.
This is the only thing that keeps some parents going."
—PHYLLIS DILLER

By the time your children are 5 years old, their brains have already reached 90% of adult size, meaning much of the basic development has already been done; however, there is *plenty* more pruning yet to occur. A majority of the pruning process during this time is driven by the new experiences of attending daycare or attending school, socializing with peers, and learning new academic skills such as reading, writing and arithmetic.

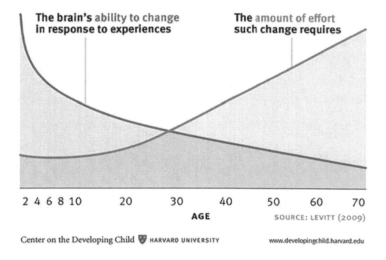

The brain's ability to change in response to experiences

The amount of effort such change requires

2 4 6 8 10   20   30   40   50   60   70

AGE   SOURCE: LEVITT (2009)

Center on the Developing Child 🛡 HARVARD UNIVERSITY   www.developingchild.harvard.edu

One interesting distinction between childhood and adolescence is that during this time your child's body will devote more energy to growing its *brain* than it will to growing its *body*. During infancy, it is the cerebellum that grows most as your child masters motor skills, but during the core years of childhood it is the *cerebrum* that most develops as your child learns how to think and reason. One need only consider how relatively easy it is for your children to learn things at this age, as compared to how *difficult* it is for adults to learn new things in middle age. If it seems like your children are "sponges" at this age… it's because they are. This is when it's easiest for them to learn material, such as a second language, while in adulthood we will always speak a second language with an accent… because our older brains can't develop the wiring as efficiently as when we're young.

Adolescence: "A Ferrari with Weak Brakes"

"When your children are teenagers, it's important to have a dog so that someone in the house is happy to see you."
—NORA EPHRON

Next we find our way to the most challenging years of parenting, the teen years. An important thing to remember about these years is that your child's behavior during this time isn't necessarily the result of some sort of character flaw on their part, nor is it a result of any mistakes you might have made as a parent. There are biological factors responsible for the awkward, clumsy behavior that your children demonstrate during these years, along with the grumpy moods.

During these years, your children's bodies devote more energy to growing physically than they do towards mental and emotional growth. The brain itself also develops from the "back" to the "front," meaning that the last part of the brain to mature is the frontal lobe—the very front of the brain—which is responsible for self-control, decision making, and empathy, among other traits.

This is why, as every adult is painfully aware, teenagers often don't make the best choices. This is when your adolescent's brain has its second (and final) neuronal "explosion," similar to the toddler years, and may actually resemble those outbursts and tantrums that you experienced back then. Adding more complexity, there is also significant pruning of the neurons that occurs as the brain optimizes itself for its particular surroundings, whatever that environment may be. This pruning helps the adolescent begin navigating the adult world, but the unfortunate flip side of this rapid brain development is that the dramatic ability to grow and learn during this phase also leaves the brain vulnerable to possible *devastating* addictions. This is why during these years a child becoming addicted to drugs, alcohol, smoking, or other destructive behaviors can cause *much* worse long-term consequences than if those behaviors were taken up in the years *after* the brain was done maturing. This is also why it is much easier for teenagers to become addicted to such substances, while adults who take up those habits later on may experience less brain damage and are less likely to become addicted. For example, an individual under age 21 who uses nicotine has a 40% risk of developing an addiction in adulthood, whereas an individual whose first exposure is after the age of 21 has a less than 10% chance of developing an addiction to nicotine.

And Into Adulthood: "... from Chaos to Clarity"

"When I was a boy of 14, my father was so ignorant
I could hardly stand to have the old man around.
But when I got to be 21, I was astonished at how
much the old man had learned in seven years."
—MARK TWAIN

Last but not least is your child's march into adulthood, and if you've survived the teenage years then feel free to give yourself a pat on the back. As the public service announcements tell everyone, it gets better.

AT WHAT AGE DO VARIOUS MENTAL POWERS PEAK?

18-19: Information processing speed

25-35: Short-term memory

30: Memory for faces

40s-50s: Emotional understanding

60s: Vocabulary

60s-70s: Accumulated knowledge and facts about the world

Source: VeryWellMind.com, with data from MIT

What's important to note here is that although the brain comes of age in the late 20s, like every other part of the body, and with the human experience in general, the 20s are not when the growth and development of the brain ends. Indeed, adulthood is a robust period marked with various peaks and valleys of development just like childhood and adolescence, rather than the protracted, morbid march of decline that we once feared that it was.

Brain Plasticity:
"The Neurons That Fire Together, Wire Together"

A key factor in understanding the up and down nature of brain development—not just its growth in childhood and adolescence but also throughout adulthood—is what science calls brain plasticity. Plasticity simply means that, as with the process in childhood of neuronal bursts and pruning, the brain grows and changes over time to optimize itself for its environment.

For example, one series of studies compared the brains of London cab drivers and bus drivers. In theory, one might expect that since people in both occupations "drive for a living" that therefore their brains might all be about the same. Yet brain scans revealed *dramatic* differences in the parts of the brain associated with direction and navigation. Although bus drivers typically drive the same route day after day, cab drivers there have to navigate on the fly one of the world's great cities. Indeed, the city's cab driver licensing exam requires drivers to learn their way around *25,000* different streets. Not surprisingly, the greatest differences in brain growth and structure were found in longtime cab drivers, whose brain scans revealed significantly larger and more developed regions for direction and navigation. With the recent advent of apps with traffic-sensitive directions, this is undoubtedly a study that would be worth revisiting.

For your children, this means that we shouldn't give up all hope should they become truly addicted to their technology. Although for centuries science was very fatalistic about the brain, believing that what you're born with can never change, today we know that over time the brain *is* capable of healing and rewiring itself. Although it sounds dramatic, that process happens *every single time* we learn something. Stroke patients are another prime example of this, as it takes time, but they're often able to relearn skills that used to be controlled by parts of their brain that were damaged by a stroke. Through the process of physical therapy and rehabilitation, their brains learn how to perform those same actions, but using the other healthy, remaining parts of the brain—no different from how, in the aftermath of a traffic accident, police will keep traffic moving by directing cars around the accident and on to side streets.

The Neurochemical Process

Important to remember about the process of neuronal explosions and pruning, along with the plasticity of the brain, is that this all takes place on a chemical level, which is what makes the brain so fascinating and complicated. Indeed, one of the frontiers of medicine today is understanding the unique chemistry of the body down to the walls of individual cells so that treatments can be designed to be as targeted and effective as possible, with as few side effects as possible. As we all know from taking various medications, a substance that fixes a problem in one part of our anatomy can create a problem elsewhere, such as when a cancer patient receives chemotherapy which also causes their hair to fall out, or when we take an antibiotic to combat an infection, which then also kills off the bacteria in our intestines that help us digest food.

An integrative approach to mental health today entails not only treatments such as therapy or behavior modification but also an understanding of the chemistry of the brain itself. Imbalances in different chemicals and hormones, down to the cellular level, can have *dramatic* effects on our mood and overall health. This is true of adults of course, but *especially* for the developing brains of children. There are several dozen neurochemicals involved in brain functions, which involve complex interactions and play various roles; however, we will focus on dopamine as a key to understanding our relationship with addictions to technology, behaviors, and substances.

Why Parenting Really Matters

Here again we come to the timeless question of nature versus nurture. That is, what most shapes humans—is it the genetic hardwiring with which we're born (nature) or is it parenting and the environment in which we are raised (nurture)?

There are plenty of arguments back and forth for each side, along with plenty of studies of identical twins who were separated at birth that seek to answer this precise question. The 2018 CNN documentary *Three Identical Strangers* explored the "nature versus nurture" argument with three identical triplets who were intentionally separated at birth and raised in separate homes around the New York City area, yet still grew up to cross their legs the same way and all smoke the same brand of cigarettes. The consensus today is that the nature versus nurture is less of a "debate" but more of a "dance."

The most current research tells us that while we each come with a set of genetic instructions, those instructions can be modified by the environment that we live in and how we interact with that environment. Like two ballroom dancers, both nature and nurture interact with each other and feed off of each other in ways that, over time, form an adult who is uniquely adapted for his or her particular environment.

8 THINGS TO REMEMBER ABOUT CHILD DEVELOPMENT:

- Even infants and young children are affected adversely when significant stresses threaten their family and caregiving environments.

- Development is a highly interactive process, and life outcomes are not determined solely by genes.

- While attachments to their parents are primary, young children can also benefit significantly from relationships with other responsive caregivers both within and outside the family.

- A great deal of brain architecture is shaped during the first three years after birth, but the window of opportunity for its development does not close on a child's third birthday.

- Severe neglect appears to be at least as great a threat to health and development as physical abuse—possibly even greater.

- Young children who have been exposed to adversity or violence do not invariably develop stress-related disorders or grow up to be violent adults.

- Simply removing a child from a dangerous environment will not automatically reverse the negative impacts of that experience.

- Resilience requires relationships, not rugged individualism.

Source: Harvard University's Center on the Developing Child

This is why parenting is so important. We all do our best to nurture our children in ways that promote a happy and healthy brain. Providing a safe and secure environment for your children's development is crucial because, as you might expect, in their younger years, your children's brains are encoding memories and experiences at a dramatic rate. The difference between a child being born into a safe and stimulating environment with nutritious food and caring adults, as opposed to unhealthy food, toxic substances, and a lack of interaction can put a child on one of two radically different life trajectories. During these earliest times, children also develop assumptions about the world, such as whether or not the world is a safe or dangerous place, and whether or not adults can be trusted. And, unfortunately, even though we all wish otherwise, the introduction of a high quality environment in later years can't necessarily compensate for whatever does and doesn't happen to a child during the earliest times of their life.

The human brain is indeed a truly marvelous creation that science has only begun to understand. We strongly believe that the parenting we provide around technology is among the most important that there is today. Similar to providing the healthiest food we can afford, a helmet for bike riding, and daily educational instruction for a healthy brain, parents today need to include appropriate technology use.

KEY TAKEAWAYS FROM THIS CHAPTER

- The brain comprises only 2% of adult body weight but consumes 20% of its energy
- Humans are born immature, with much brain development occurring after birth
- The brain develops through a series of neuron "bursts" in which brain cells grow and expand, followed by periods of "pruning" in which unused cells / connections wither away
- The brain matures from the back to the front, with self-restraint and decision making among the last skills to be developed.
- Nature and nurture act together to adapt a child's brain to his or her environment

FOR FURTHER READING

- *The Teenage Brain: A Neuroscientist's Survival Guide to Raising Adolescents and Young Adults* by Dr. Frances Jensen
- *The Glass Cage: How Our Computers are Changing Us* by Nicholas Carr
- *The Shallows: What the Internet is Doing to Our Brains* by Nicholas Carr

CHAPTER FOUR

Process Addictions and the Brain

"There's no such thing as addiction,
there's only things that you enjoy doing more than life."
—DOUG STANHOPE

THE HUMAN BRAIN IS INDEED A MARVEL OF NATURE, BUT unfortunately that marvel doesn't exist in a vacuum, nor was it designed to exist in a vacuum. Like a mighty sailing ship, our brains weren't designed to sit in a dry dock. They're designed to help us navigate the world, and as we covered through the process of neuronal growth and pruning, our brains *adapt* to their environment over time. Unfortunately, that ability to adapt has a downside, in that it leaves our brains vulnerable to both harmful substances and behaviors despite negative outcomes. This is why we call the latter "process" addictions.

What Motivates Us

"I love blackjack. But I'm not addicted to gambling
I'm addicted to sitting in a semicircle."
—MITCH HEDBERG

As we navigate the world, the forces we encounter will typically either cause us to be attracted to or repulsed by something, often to the very core of our beings. Our brains are instinctively, intuitively repulsed by rotten food or fearful of extreme heights, but we are also instinctively, intuitively drawn to the delicious smell of a freshly cooked meal or feel safe with our feet firmly planted on the ground. This basic building block of the study of human behavior is what psychologists call approach-avoidance behaviors, as we *approach* some things, while we *avoid* others.

Mother Nature has some very legitimate reasons for that innate programming. A freshly cooked meal will provide us with a good source of nutrition and having our feet planted firmly on the ground will go a long way towards sustaining life, as our ancestors who followed those edicts generally stood a good chance of surviving and reproducing the species. On the other hand, rotten food can be full of any number of diseases or poisons, while a bad encounter with extreme heights may not end well, and in both cases our ancestors who let those curiosities get the best of them probably weren't able to pass their genes on to the next generation. This is why, one generation after another, we've been hardwired as a species to *approach* some things while we *avoid* others, and the study of those divergent actions has been a key foundation to the understanding of human behavior.

That basic programming works well most of the time, but things go awry if substances and behaviors hijack those instincts. For example, although it might feel good initially to consume illegal drugs, over time those drugs will destroy our bodies, and thus society has laws to keep those drugs out of circulation. Even more common, we approach fast food because it tastes good going down and we're conditioned to crave the sugar, salt, and fat that's rare in the natural world but packed into those "foods," yet we know to avoid eating too much fast food because of its disastrous health consequences. Today, of course, we might all enjoy—"approach"—checking social media, but doing so all day long at the office isn't exactly the best way to climb the corporate ladder. but due to the lack of *immediate* negative consequences, we don't necessarily learn right away to avoid overusing social media.

Substances like drugs and food are obvious perpetrators whereas addictions related to things we do, such as gambling, shopping, eating, and technology are addictions that are defined as process addictions. With process addictions it is the *behavior* that our brains feel compelled to continue despite the potential negative impact that occurs in every facet of our lives.

Fortunately, we all have free will, but sometimes overriding those natural instincts, when it comes to addictive substances or behaviors, can be difficult for some. This is primarily due to a key neurochemical in the brain—dopamine.

Dopamine—"The Kardashian of Molecules"

As we touched on briefly in the previous chapter, dopamine is one of the most powerful neurochemicals that influence the reward center in our brain.

Whenever we anticipate pleasure, dopamine lights up our brains, and a crucial trigger in addiction is just *how much* dopamine is released. For example, cocaine has been shown to release *10 times* the amount of dopamine in the brain as normal enjoyable activities like eating food or having sex. This is precisely why addictions are so dangerous—because of their ability to flood the brain with neurochemicals such that people lose control over their behavior—as the comedian Doug Stanhope said, when some people enjoy certain things more than living itself. The difference is that most of our daily activities like cooking dinner, paying the bills, or driving to work aren't exactly going to arouse our senses in the way that those pleasurable activities will—as that's what makes them pleasurable.

Research today shows that chronic technology use lights up the brain in a similar way that many other addictions do. As we explained earlier, it's not so much either the substance or the behavior that's the danger but *how it affects the brain.* Furthermore, chronic technology use from childhood onward is now being shown to affect those neurochemical pathways *just like traditional substances and other behavioral addictions do* in a way that can possibly prime the brain from an early age for a *lifetime* of addiction.

Rewards—"The *Pursuit* is the Reward"

"The quickest way to double your money playing the lottery is to fold it in half and put it back in your pocket."
—INTERNET JOKE

So now we come to the point where all of that fancy science of the previous chapters all starts to make sense.

One additional key principle in understanding human behavior is the concept of reinforcement. Whenever we perform one behavior, the consequences that we receive constitute either a reinforcement (good) or punishment (bad) and as you can imagine, within the brain itself dopamine is the *ultimate* reinforcement.

In the broader world, the reinforcements you would receive from going to work, for example, would include not only your paycheck but also intangibles like esteem from peers, praise from your supervisor, and a sense of contributing to the world, to say nothing of being able to pay your bills, live your life, and provide for your family. Opposite of reinforcement is punishment, which in a work context we all know would include being fired, reprimanded, written up, docked pay or demoted, or simply being shunned by colleagues and professional organizations. Those positive and negative consequences, above and beyond our neurochemical reactions, are ways that our behavior can be incentivized both for better and for worse, by both internal and external forces.

One key way to manipulate behavior is in the timeline in which those rewards are delivered—or not delivered—along with the magnitude of those rewards. Humans respond to four types of reward "schedules"—fixed or variable intervals (the time between rewards) along with a fixed or variable ratio (number of responses). For example, if you go to work and are paid regularly with the same predictable, flat, consistent wage, then you will typically perform a certain way, as you're being paid on a fixed interval schedule. But if you go to work and are suddenly paid twice your regular wage, then you're being paid on a variable ratio. It's one thing to discuss this sort of thing in the abstract, but it's another matter entirely to see a mouse in a cage tap a lever over and over and over and over again, receiving—or not receiving—rewards of different sizes and in different intervals. We humans are no different, as we all know how differently sales agents can behave when they're paid on commission as opposed to being paid a flat wage, just as we all know the joy or disappointment that comes from potential end of year bonuses or lack thereof.

As you can imagine, this uncertainty messes with your mind rather quickly. This is exactly how slot machines in casinos work—you put in money, pull the lever, and don't know what will happen—and it's also *exactly* how your technology is being designed (minus the free alcohol and buffet, of course). Science today tells us that with these sorts of variable reward schedules, the rush of dopamine comes from the *anticipation* of the reward, rather than the actual reward itself. Another classic example here is that of lottery winners. Although we all might enjoy playing the lottery every once in a while, particularly when the jackpots get big, the neurochemical rush comes from buying the tickets, perhaps joining a pool at the office, or watching television as the winning numbers are announced to the public. On a rare occasion, some people *do* win the lottery, which undoubtedly releases the sort of dopamine that we can all only imagine. But even after that burst, as many studies have shown, life for many people *after* they've won the lottery is often anything but pleasant, suggesting that it's the anticipation and not the win.

Casinos of course are famous for having little old ladies sit in front of slot machines for days upon end, feeding those machines with endless streams of quarters; this is exactly the sort of reward system that's being designed into our technology. Some estimates today say that the average American checks his or her phone 180 times a day, which to us doesn't seem as unimaginable as it might sound. The variable rewards here leave us forever anticipating that next hit of dopamine from that next email, that next text message, that next like of a Facebook post, or continuation of a Snapchat streak. And, just like the casinos, our phones are full of flashing lights and pretty colors. We haven't heard of any machines in casinos that vibrate when you use them… although that's undoubtedly in the pipeline somewhere.

The concern for us as psychologists and parents—a key motivation in writing this book—was that it's bad enough that these techniques are being built into devices for adults—casinos and lotteries rightfully exclude those under 18 years of age—but that they're also being built into devices for our children. The repeated hit of dopamine that our brains get from checking our devices is something that quite possibly is priming the brains of our children for a lifetime of addiction—just like the smoker or drinker who can resume his or her habit all too easily after years of abstinence—leaving them vulnerable in ways that we're only beginning to understand. And although we don't yet know how dangerous this may be, we do know that the brain never forgets.

What is Addiction?

"Today, 62 percent of 18- to 24-year-olds have their cell phones with them 90 percent of the time. And Americans send 18.7 billion text messages every month. I think my 15 year old daughter may be responsible for 18.6 billion of them!"
—KATIE COURIC, 2007 Williams College commencement speech

Central to any addiction is the loss of control over one's behavior, whether due to a substance or a process like gambling or shopping. Addiction has been studied extensively in the scientific community over the last 50 years (as we noted in our opening chapters, things are far worse even than when Katie Couric gave the above speech), and much of it applies to our interactions with technology today.

Symptoms of addiction, broadly speaking, include the inability of a person to stop using the offending substance or engage in the offending behavior regardless of the consequences. Similar to an individual who continues to smoke cigarettes despite being diagnosed with lung cancer or emphysema (and its many effects on their health and finances), individuals struggling with the process addiction of gambling will continue to gamble despite being late on their mortgages or being on the brink of bankruptcy.

The effects of addiction can be devastating—comedian Doug Stanhope's joke at the beginning of the chapter about people choosing an addiction rather than living their lives is simultaneously funny and yet painfully tragic, as anyone who's had a loved one battle an addiction knows all too well. As we noted earlier, substance and process addictions have been with us for centuries, which is why governments go to such great lengths to contain and control them, and that's why we need to rein in our technology use today.

Hijacking the Structure of the Brain

Like a terrorist seizing the controls of an aircraft and holding the flight crew and passengers hostage, or a virus that infects a cell and turns it into a factory to produce more viruses, addictions take over the brain in any number of insidious ways that research is only beginning to understand, devastating both our brains and our lives in the process.

Atrophy of Gray Matter. Gray matter is where much of the heavy duty processing takes place in the brain—comprising only 40% of cells yet consuming 94% of the brain's oxygen. These cells are more than a bit important to our functioning, and yet multiple studies have shown atrophy (shrinkage) or loss of tissue volume in the gray matter area of the brain in "high level" (more than 3 hours per day) gamers. Areas affected include the frontal lobe (executive functions such as planning, prioritizing tasks, organizing, and impulse control) and the parts of the brain that develop empathy and compassion for others. These parts of the brain dictate the depth and quality of personal relationships, and their deterioration makes us vulnerable to aggressive behavior, as we'll illustrate later in one of our case studies.

Compromised White Matter. In the interior of the brain is the white matter that connects gray matter and makes complex, multidimensional thinking possible. Research of multiple-hour gamers is now showing a loss of integrity in white matter cells, interrupting connections, slowing down the transmission of nerve impulses, and short circuiting communications across the brain. In English, this means kids who are impacted might struggle with making decisions, controlling impulses, and managing their emotions.

Taken together, we shouldn't be surprised that the above adds up to less efficient information processing within the brain, along with a reduced impulse inhibition, increased sensitivity to gaining rewards, and insensitivity to the loss of rewards. While these outcomes do not present in *every* heavy user of technology, technology overuse can have important and significant adverse effects on the brain of children who spend their days endlessly connected to electronic devices—no different than those compulsive gamblers who haunt the casinos of Las Vegas and Atlantic City.

Okay, So What Do We Do About It?

"You pile up enough tomorrows, and you'll find you are left with nothing but a lot of empty yesterdays."
—FROM THE MUSICAL *THE MUSIC MAN*

If you're reading this book, then you're probably navigating the challenges of technology saturation in your family, fearful that a loved one may be headed down that path of overuse or addiction, or you work with children and adults facing the possibility. Odds are that we can all agree it's a problem.

Unfortunately, a common perception today is that a person has to "hit rock bottom" with an addiction before beginning the process of recovery, whether it's alcoholics who lose their jobs and families or students who flunk out of college because they played video games all day long and never studied or went to class. We can all agree we wouldn't want our children to hit rock bottom with technology.

So now we pivot away from much of what you've long suspected—that technology overuse is a problem—and focus on the *real* reason why you bought this book—solutions. It's time for Goldilocks to find her Zone.

Give yourself credit for buying this book in the first place. As we noted, the first step in *solving* any problem is to *recognize* that there is one. For some, hopefully, this book might be helpful in *preventing* the problem in the first place. With that in mind, we believe that the key to solving a problem is a systematic approach—breaking down the problem into its component parts and addressing those issues both individually and holistically to create the change necessary for a happy, healthy, and productive life—both for you *and* your children.

KEY TAKEAWAYS FROM THIS CHAPTER

- Human behavior is best explained in terms of what we approach and what we avoid.

- The neurochemical dopamine is key to understanding addiction, and the manipulation of the brain's dopamine release is key to the biology of addiction.

- Science today is uncovering just how devastating addictions can be to anatomy of the brain.

- The science of addiction has advanced dramatically in recent decades, such that mental health professionals can now understand technology overuse through both behavior *and* brain functioning.

FOR FURTHER READING

- *Hooked: How to Build Habit Forming Products*, by Nir Eyal
- *Invisible Influence: The Hidden Forces That Shape Behavior*, by Jonah Berger

SECTION TWO
The Four Dimensions of Technology Addiction

CHAPTER FIVE

Assessing Your Child's Technology Use

"Parenthood is an amazing opportunity
to be able to ruin someone from scratch."
—JON STEWART

W E ALL KNOW INSTINCTIVELY THAT A SKINNED KNEE IS
not the same thing as a broken bone. A skinned knee might need
to be washed and cleaned, covered with a band-aid, and kissed to make it
better, but a high fever or a broken bone can require a visit to the family
doctor if not the emergency room. As new parents, we all have a tendency
to overthink every success or failure our child has along with every cough
or cold symptom, but with time and experience we understand the many
shades of gray in both their behavior and their development. That's why the
tools we'll be outlining in this chapter operate on a continuum, and not in
black and white.

The problem with issues like technology overuse, as well as the broader
issue of healthy living, is that it's often difficult to separate particular maladies
from the normal ups and downs of childhood. Although the exact terminology ("technology addiction," "gaming disorder," etc.) and diagnostic criteria
are still being debated and refined, you wouldn't be reading this book and we

wouldn't be writing it if this were not an issue today. If your house is burning down, you don't care what make and model the fire trucks are, only that they can bring the water needed to put out the fire.

As we all know, the stigma long associated with any sort of mental health-care (typically the first line of treatment for any sort of addiction) prevents many adults from getting the help we all need from time to time. In the case of both physical and mental health, regular checkups are the best way to ensure a happy and healthy life over the long run, no matter what life throws at us. As parents, we don't hesitate to get our kids glasses or braces as needed, and yet, given the stunning complexities of the brain that we only scratched the surface of in the last chapter, it's amazing to us as professionals that so many mental health issues are still today are either written off as character flaws or deemed not worthy of treatment. Addressing problems with your child's brain chemistry—along with outside forces designed to exploit it—is a difficult row to hoe, and we know because *we see it every day.*

This is a Problem That *Can* Be Solved

Every day in our practices we work with parents worried that their children are in need of treatment at a residential facility like the Betty Ford Clinic just because their kids text and play video games all day long. And while those facilities do exist for technology overuse, like any sort of mental health hospitalization, they're a *dramatic* last option. The *vast* majority of parents and children can find meaningful, happy, satisfying outcomes by doing the dirty work of managing their technology issues on a daily basis without the "nuclear option" of inpatient care, in the same way that most physical ailments can be treated with measures short of open heart or brain surgery. Like other personal problems (diet, exercise, work/life balance, etc.), it's simply something that we have to work on a little bit every day. Parents need to remember that sending a child to a treatment facility can be *very* stressful not only for the child but for the family, to say nothing of the outrageous costs of American healthcare today.

We understand your concerns. We see them *every single day*, both at work and at home. But, as we'll unpack throughout the rest of the book, we believe that there are many, many effective ways to manage technology overuse short of the dramatic step of residential treatment.

Most clinicians today treat technology overuse using the models of drug and alcohol abuse; as you'll note throughout the book, there's a good deal of overlap in the *biology* of substance and process addictions, but in our years of experience we've come to believe that they require different *treatment approaches*. In particular, we've come to believe that technology uniquely affects our children in four different areas—their behavior, their physical health, their emotional wellbeing, and their interpersonal skills. As you'll see, we've designed our assessments and interventions around those four areas, which we'll outline in the next few chapters. However, first let's start with assessing your child's risk for technology overuse.

Introducing the Technology Use Continuum (TUC)

Breaking down your child's relationship with technology into its behavioral, physical, emotional, and interpersonal elements is at the heart of our "Technology Use Continuum" (or "TUC"), which we've designed to empower parents and other caretakers with a simple and easy to understand tool for evaluating their child's technology use.

Behavioral factors are observable ways in which your child conducts him or herself on a daily basis. This section of the TUC asks you to evaluate your child's behavior as it relates to their ability to put down their technology and prioritize school work, sports, and extra-curriculars while keeping video games and online streaming limited to their proper role as leisure activities.

Physical symptoms are the often overlooked basic elements of your children's physical appearance as well as diet and exercise. TUC questions here ask you to evaluate your children's amount of sleep, whether or not they seem tired all the time, how much exercise they're getting, if they complain about physical discomfort, whether they're over or underweight, and whether or not they consume heavy amounts of energy drinks or other caffeinated beverages.

Emotional symptoms refer to the moods of your child both when using or away from technology, as well as how separation from technology affects how he or she feels about the world. TUC questions here ask you to evaluate whether your child experiences periods of unusual sadness or anger, is emotionally withdrawn, demonstrates an improved mood following technology use, or experiences dramatic swings in mood.

Lastly, **interpersonal symptoms** refers to the quality of your child's social life and ability to connect with other people. TUC questions here ask you to evaluate whether or not your child can interact successfully with adults and other children, whether most of your child's friends are online, and whether or not there's conflict in the household over technology use.

Taken together, the TUC provides a good preliminary screening device for just how much your child is using, overusing, or addicted to technology. As you'll see, we've developed several versions of the TUC to use depending on your child's age. Think of the TUC along the lines of taking your child's temperature or looking at an eye chart. Your child's use of technology will continually change over time, but using the TUC to evaluate them from time to time will help you identify that healthy balance you want. That wiggle room we're looking for between living off of the grid and spending our days endlessly connected to technology—that's our Goldilocks Zone.

Technology Use Continuums for children of various ages can be found in the Appendix

---

Analyze Your Child's Screen Time

After first getting the big picture as to whether or not your child presents symptoms of technology overuse with the TUC, if you're still concerned, we recommend moving on to the second step of documenting and then analyzing your child's device usage with either common screen time programs or with a technology use log.

It's important to note that your child can disproportionately overuse one particular piece of technology yet still otherwise have a perfectly balanced, healthy relationship with technology in general. A technology use log will allow you to begin to "drill down" and evaluate what particular pieces of technology your child is using, when they are using them, and why. Using a graphing calculator for advanced math homework, for example, is not the same thing as playing mindless video games, and we shouldn't treat it as such.

A SAMPLE TECHNOLOGY USE LOG

Technology	Time	Total Minutes	Purpose
computer	1:00	45 minutes	homework

If you are unable to monitor your child's technology use in person, there are excellent programs for tracking technology use available on the Internet for various platforms. These tools will allow you to document and analyze your child's computer usage, and many will now provide reports back to you via email. We encourage you to speak with your cellular or Internet provider, or utilize highly rated 3rd party apps reviewed in Consumer Reports or on CNET.com.

We recommend starting by tracking your child's use on as typical a day as possible, including at least one representative day during the week and another representative day on the weekend. For example, if your child has sports practice on Monday nights but every other night of the week is spent at home on the computer, then Mondays won't be reflective of your child's overall schedule.

Once you've captured a relative snapshot of your child's technology use, we then recommend tracking their device use over an entire week, if possible.

Create Structure and Expectations with Technology Use Contracts

Once you understand what technology your children are using and to what degree, the next step is to codify what kind of relationship you want your children to have with their technology going forward. The best way to do this is with technology use contracts as, just like contracts in the adult world, they can spell out your expectations for your children as well as the rewards and consequences for their behavior, which you can then amend over time as your children grow. Remember, *children rise and fall to the level of expectations that we have for them.*

A SAMPLE TECHNOLOGY USAGE CONTRACT

[Johnny / Susie] agrees to not use his/her cellphone between the hours of 10pm and 7am unless specifically granted permission by mom and dad. If [Johnny / Susie] uses his/her cell phone during those prohibited hours, he/she will turn in his/her cellphone to mom/dad for one/two/three days.

Writing a technology use contract with your children is an excellent opportunity for them to participate in establishing boundaries and guidelines for technology use in your household. If your children want to hold you to a similar contract (as we'll discuss in the chapter on distracted parenting), talk with them about it and be open to the possibility. For fun, you can even have your "contracts" witnessed by a relative or friend and then framed on the wall or hung on the refrigerator as a way to remind everyone in the household what they've all agreed upon. This will all help create the buy-in you'll need to enforce these rules over the long term to create healthy norms for everyone.

Keep in mind also that, kids being kids, they'll do everything they can to wiggle out of every little clause of whatever contracts you write. Language is an imperfect expression of human thought and for that reason we recommend having relatives or close friends read over your "contracts" to anticipate any unintended loopholes that could become an issue later on. For example, one family we advised had a son who was an active middle school wrestler. In the technology use contract they'd all agreed to, a third violation of his usage would result in being suspended from his school's wrestling team for one week. When he violated the contract for a third time, his parents were ready to suspend him from the team. He did in fact have an important wrestling competition that weekend, but it was under the banner of his private club team rather than his school team, meaning that in the strictest interpretation of his contract, his parents couldn't punish him as intended. Although he was allowed to compete at the meet that weekend, that came on the condition that he and his parents would amend their ongoing contract.

Preliminary Strategies for Managing Common Devices

Computers. First and foremost, we recommend that parents never locate a computer or television set in their children's bedroom. Doing so grants children a virtual "candy store" of information that even the best filtering software can't prevent them from seeing, particularly once you're asleep. As your children will always be one step ahead of you with technology, you'll want them using their devices when adults are around to monitor whatever media it is that they're consuming.

THE DARK SIDE OF BLUE LIGHT

Today's screens are known for emitting "blue light," a particular wavelength in the light spectrum. Blue light is released during the day by the sun and is known to boost attention, reaction times, and mood. During the day of course that's exactly what our bodies need, but our bodies aren't built for the artificial nighttime lights that civilization has given us in the last few hundred years. That light has been shown to interfere with the body's natural circadian rhythms due to a hormone known as melatonin.

THE DRACULA OF HORMONES—MELATONIN

Like Count Dracula, melatonin is known for only coming out at night, and you could say that it packs just as much of a bite. Melatonin is the hormone that is key not only to restful sleep, but also to the ability to fall asleep at all. The blue light released at night by our electronic devices impedes the body's natural release of melatonin, which is a nice way of saying that the longer we stare at our screens at night, the more difficulty we have falling asleep, let alone enjoying high quality sleep.

The American Academy of Pediatrics (AAP) traditionally recommended no more than two hours of screen time per day, preferably high quality content. However, the AAP is now steering clear of screen time limits, over the age of 5, and encouraging more thoughtful screen time planning. Obviously, the more time your children spend in front of screens, the less time they have to play outside, read books, engage in hobbies, or simply let their imaginations run wild. The recommendation of two hours also takes into account the physical, developmental, and emotional consequences of too much screen time. However, we're quite realistic and before you panic, remember that every child is unique and that the limits you set should be guided by the individual needs of your child, the quality of the content your child consumes, and the particular problems with technology use that you're having. For example, your 4th grader might only get two hours of technology use… but that could be unrealistic for your 10th grader.

Keep in mind also that "high quality" online content can change from year to year and can also vary depending on the age of your children. Since we recommend no screens before the age of 2, the best content recommendations after that age will come from parents with older children along with your children's teachers. Some schools today are also able to negotiate discounted rates on pay websites for educational programming as well.

Smartphones and Tablets. The smarter the device, the older your child should be to own it. As people all around the world know today, phones with Internet access can be one of the biggest distractions for everyone, not just children. Providing your child with a smartphone can lead to less sleep and excessive usage due to both the addictive properties of the device and its various apps, along with the same problem of blue light that other electronic screens also have. We recommend never allowing your child access to a cell phone with an Internet connection in their room, most especially at night. Without supervision, your children will be able to send messages and play video games at all hours of the night, possibly getting their way around any filtering software you've installed.

We recommend not giving your children a phone in elementary school as children that young are typically too immature for the responsibilities and privileges that come from owning such a device. High school is a more ideal time to get your child this device, which makes middle school the typical battleground for parents today. Should you absolutely need to get your child a cell phone in either grade school or middle school, we strongly recommend getting your child a basic flip phone—and nothing more—that will allow them to call and text with you but avoid the dangers of unsupervised access to more mature content.

On entering middle school and high school, kids will typically want access to a smartphone, and for kids on the younger end of that age bracket we recommend writing up technology use contracts. A good technology use contract should stipulate that your child will not use his or her phone during class, extra-curriculars, or any important family time (religious services, family dinners, etc.), and that you as a parent will be monitoring their access with the parental guards and monitoring tools that your service provider offers. This will allow you to prevent a good deal of the cyberbullying, illegal transfer of files, etc. that we'll discuss in greater detail later in the book. And if your child still hasn't demonstrated the maturity to handle a smartphone, feel free to stick with the flip phone.

Video Games. As mentioned above, we recommend keeping video game consoles out in the common areas of your household rather than in a child's bedroom, and that you also use timers to limit their time on these devices. That said, unlike the video game consoles you may have grown up with, today's gaming systems typically come with Internet connections that allow users to connect with people all over the world. This not only opens your children up to possible online predators, particularly given how naive children can be, but the 24/7 global availability of games means that your kids can quite easily stay up all night playing games with other players around the world who might be playing on a day off from school, in the middle of the afternoon. This makes it that much more possible for your children to be sucked into the dangerous world of some of today's endless video games (the ones designed to not have an ending) and even more detached from the real world.

Television/Streaming. Despite the generation gap in traditional television viewership, kids today are nonetheless drawn to programming long before entering school, if only because we adults have a tendency to leave it on in the background. Some reports indicate that fully two thirds of infants and toddlers today watch an average of three hours of programming per day, with that usage increasing to four hours per day by age 8. Adding in video games and the Internet, the average 8 year old today is spending as much as 6 hours per day looking at screens, although this will probably increase as online video and music streaming build critical mass in the marketplace.

We support the AAPs' recommendation of no digital programming whatsoever for children under the age of 2. For children from 2 years of age up to middle school, the best case scenario is no more than one to two hours of quality programming per day. However, we are realistic given remote learning environments, global pandemics, and the incessant demands of our children. As with other screens, the more time children spend watching programs, the less time they have for the play and social interaction critical to their physical and social development. It's about balance!

Studies show that children with access to programming in their bedrooms, not surprisingly, sleep less than the average child. Children who are sleep deprived, no matter what age, struggle with regulating emotions, and weight. In addition to the television rating system company tools that will allow you to censor your child's programming, we recommend consulting websites such as IMDB (the Internet Movie Database) and TVGuidelines.org for more detailed information about the programming your children are watching, and to ensure that the content meshes with your family's particular values.

Don't Forget to Keep Perspective

"I don't know what's more exhausting about parenting; the getting up early, or acting like you know what you're doing."
—JIM GAFFIGAN

As we discuss throughout the book, as parents we all need to remember that our children are continually growing and developing. Their behavior, like their brains, isn't set in stone. Your child's brain will continue to grow and change not only in childhood but also throughout adulthood as it adapts to its environment. So although your child may have a higher TUC score in middle school or high school, that can very easily change over time. It can be easy to overreact to every little thing your child does, but don't give in to panic. Step back, relax, use the tools and recommendations we give you, and, more often than not, things will turn out just fine. Something that's a problem at age 12 may be a running joke among all of you when your children are grown.

And Be Consistent!

For better and for worse, one of our children's greatest strengths is that they have sharp, built-in B.S. detectors. They know when we're trying to pull a fast one on them. With technology, as with household rules in general, rules aren't rules if there aren't any consequences. Your children will pick up rather quickly if you and their other caretakers are lax in enforcing rules, so don't be ɩfraid to use your backbone from time to time to remind them of who is in charge. Remember that your children have friends; what they need from you is to be their parent.

In our experience working with schools and giving countless presentations, we've found time and time again that our kids *do* want to make the right decision, and when they do so, they should be praised and rewarded. Remember that for every mistake we catch, our children have made 1000 good decisions. If our children only ever hear criticism from us, that's a formula for fragile self-esteem. The combination of criticism and consequences, along with a healthy dose of praise *when earned,* will help them develop a healthy sense of direction, empowerment, and accomplishment that will carry them long past their childhood days. That's our Goldilocks Zone—for life.

KEY TAKEAWAYS FROM THIS CHAPTER

- Technology overuse *can* be solved without resorting to residential treatment facilities.

- Technology overuse affects children in their behavior, physical health, emotional wellbeing, and interpersonal skills.

- Our Technology Use Continuum can be used as a screening and follow-up method for assessing risk for technology overuse.

- Technology use logs help identify you and your child's current use.

- Technology use contracts codify your expectations for technology use in the family.

ACTION STEPS

- Take a snapshot of each of your children's technology use and compare it to the TUC relevant to their age.

- If you feel that your children have a problem, monitor their use of specific devices with a technology use log.

- Create structure and expectations for your children with technology use contracts, customized to each child's needs.

- Allow your children to participate in the creation of rules and norms for technology use around the house as a way to empower them and create buy-in.

- Remember that your child's technology use will change over time, both as your child matures and as technology changes. So too, you will have to change.

- Revisit the TUC for your children with time.

CHAPTER SIX

Behavioral Factors

"Teenagers complain there's nothing to do,
then stay out all night doing it."
—BOB PHILLIPS

FIRST UP ON OUR TUC, AND MOST EASILY OBSERVABLE FOR parents and caretakers, is our children's behavioral symptoms. Kids of course will use their devices for hours on end if left unsupervised, in the same way that they want to stay at a friend's birthday party until long after it's over, watch TV and stream content forever, or play with their favorite toy. This much is normal behavior.

Where we cross the line into concern is when our kids are unable to let go of technology and refuse to turn off the video games and come to dinner, or insist on playing the same game over and over again. As we mentioned earlier, in our school presentations we have videos of infants who break down crying along with toddlers who become hysterical when denied the use of their favorite devices. Remember the biology outlined in chapters three and four—there's a clinical basis for your children's reactions, and today's devices are designed around an understanding of the brain, leaving developing brains particularly at risk. If you notice that conversations with your children seem to endlessly revolve around technology—and you can't seem to find them without it—then these are some classic signs of technology overuse.

Signs and Symptoms

A good way to evaluate your children's behavior with technology is to contrast it with their behavior away from technology—the time that they spend at the dinner table, out in the neighborhood playing with friends, or playing youth sports like soccer or baseball. Like our own little science fair projects, this is the "control" baseline for our children's behavior, as contrasted with the "variable" of when they're on their phones or playing video games. The gap between their "control" behavior and their "variable" behavior will give you some insight into just how much technology is affecting them.

As clinicians, we're trained in informative ways to observe behaviors in children, but it is a bit more difficult when you've come home from a long day at work and have to cook dinner, check to see if your kids did their homework, and take the dog for a walk, to say nothing of when your husband comes home from hockey and asks you to wash his gear. Suffice to say, it can be hard to face off rationally with your child (even after throwing your spouse in the penalty box) when in the back of your mind you expect a temper tantrum the moment you ask your child to turn off their phone for the night. Unfortunately, that knee-jerk reaction from your child is *exactly* the kind of behavioral symptom of technology overuse to look for, so let's unpack those symptoms further. We'll also end the hockey metaphors with this period.

Mismanagement of Time

Children of course are not exactly masters of time management like adult professionals and executives, but one clear sign of the distortive effects of technology overuse is in how your children use or don't use their time. Although we all have free will, unfortunately we all know how easily sidetracked our kids can be with whatever interests and entertains them, and technology is no exception.

Increased Demand for Screen Time. Even if you establish healthy boundaries with technology for your children from infancy, a key sign of creeping overuse is that they'll hassle you for more and more time with their technology. However, with an increased demand for remote or virtual learning our children also have legitimate academic needs for more screen time, making it all the more challenging as parents to know where to draw the line. We need to consider the 2 hour recommendation as an additional 2 hours, over and above electronic use for school. We consider this their entertainment time. However, when you refuse to grant them this extra time or they continually ask for more time this is a sure sign that you're crossing a threshold into unhealthy overuse.

Amount of Time Spent on Technology. When your child begins to use up all of his or her free time on devices, such that it crowds out other activities like playing in the yard with friends or going to the park, or doing schoolwork, this is a second sign of technology overuse. The kids we're talking about here will seem inseparable from their devices—walking around the house doing chores, while riding in the car with you, or while sitting in the same room... and looking at their device the whole time.

Losing Track of Time / Inability to Manage Time. When your children spend hours and hours playing video games and forget to do their homework or don't give themselves enough time to do their homework (particularly older children), this is another sign of technology overuse. Here a child's first instinct is to run home and turn on the video games, or to spend hours streaming videos, while neglecting chores until it's already bedtime. They might tell you that they didn't realize the time when you ask them why they haven't started their chores or homework. While all children will lose track of time, it is an issue when this occurs more often than not every single week.

Trying to Push Back Bedtime. When your kids try to brush off being tired, even when presenting with symptoms of fatigue like circles under their eyes or irritability, and would instead prefer to spend their time playing video games, chatting with friends, etc. this is another sign that the technology has taken over their lives. Kids here will fight with you every night over bedtime, just like they'll want to jump right on their technology in the morning before even eating breakfast.

Changes in School Performance

Decline in Grades. Although not every child is a natural A+ student, if your child's grades change, particularly if they decline dramatically over time, this is another painful sign that your child is spending too much time on technology. Getting notes or calls home from teachers, missing assignments, and poor testing are all typical markers here. Be careful not to let this go on for any length of time, as it can be *very* difficult for children to make up work or improve grades, even with summer school classes. Typically, this does not result in a child's being held back in school; however, in dramatic cases, when a child is held back in middle school, it can be devastating for the family.

Missing School. If your child is skipping classes or feigning illness a la *Ferris Bueller*, this is another sign, particularly if both parents are working. Today, Ferris, Cameron, and Sloane could very well spend their day playing video games rather than seeing the sights of Chicago. And unlike the lovely but gullible parents of Ferris Bueller, be sure to verify your child's attendance online on occasion. Children with legitimate technology addiction might be dropped off at school by their parents but slip out the side door to go back home to start gaming. Schools today are much better about notifying parents of excessive absences, but parents shouldn't wait until the school notifies them of their child's attendance problems. For example, we had an elementary student forward her mother's phone to a Google line so she wouldn't get caught by her mother when she skipped school to play video games. Incredibly, the student answered the school's call and thanked them for checking in on her "sick" child. After this call, the young woman turned off the call forwarding… and her mother was none the wiser.

Tensions with Friends and Family

Increased Conflict with Family Members. Children typically feel most safe at home, and since we "hurt the ones we love," this manifests itself through a lack of patience with siblings and parents, eye rolling, and feeling entitled to screen time, all of which can culminate in temper tantrums and—at worst—physical violence, as we'll talk about later in the book. Other signs to look for include having your kids talk back to you in disrespectful ways and arguments between the technology-addicted child and his or her siblings. The child may even be quick to anger over innocent questions such as, "How was your day," or being asked to take out the garbage. This increased conflict is especially likely to occur when a device is in the child's hand. One of the many reasons this occurs is that when we ask questions of our children and they are distracted by their devices, they feel that we're interrupting them. We all know how irritating it can be to be interrupted by office colleagues or to be drawn away by our children from completing a household chore. This sense of irritation is the same for our children when interrupted from looking at their social media feeds.

Spending Less Time with Friends or Siblings. When your children want to spend all of their free time on their technology and avoid socializing in person with other kids, this too is another sign of technology overuse. Children here will typically have fewer sleepovers, spend less time at friends' houses, or no longer even mention their friends at all. When you or other caretakers raise the issue, your kids will demonstrate indifference to spending time with friends, particularly if you don't directly encourage it. Unfortunately, this is when your contact with your children can be reduced to telling them (sometimes rather strongly) to, "FIND SOMETHING TO DO!"

WHAT'S THE RIGHT BALANCE FOR A CHILD'S FRIENDS?

Ideal: active group of friends "in real life"

Acceptable: mix of online and real life friends

Be Worried: only online friends

Lying and Deceiving Friends and Adults. Children here will lie about having already done their homework, about having homework in the first place, and about what they're doing in their room. They will lie to their friends about why they can't hang out together or offer excuses to stay home and avoid watching their siblings' sports or performances / recitals so they can spend time on their devices. They might lie about who they are talking to online or who they are playing with in an online game. In other words, they lie to cover their tracks and spend more time on technology. This is similar to the alcoholic who stumbles around drunk and has bottles of booze hidden in all of the places that he or she spends time. That's not an accident.

Shifts in Interests

Loss of Interest in Sports. Given how important sports are to so many American children, kids here who might've genuinely enjoyed participating in Little League, soccer, or Pop Warner football will look to avoid going to practice, feign injuries, say that it isn't fun anymore, or complain about team-mates and coaches. Although kids often lose interest in some activities over time—this typically happens in middle school—the substitution of healthy participation in school and park district teams with endless connection to devices is something that needs to be watched over time. It's easy to relent and let your child drop out of organized activities (especially since you're the one responsible for hauling them around everywhere), but decreasing outside interests should be measured against time spent on electronic devices.

Abandonment of Hobbies. As with participation in sports, the abandonment of your kids' other longtime hobbies—anything from board games or collecting baseball cards to visiting a local park—can be a sign of overuse of technology. If your children are dropping these personality quirks of theirs in favor of increased screen time—now claiming that they're boring or uninteresting—then this is another sign to look out for.

Of course, no child will present with all of these symptoms simultaneously, and to be sure, all children will have at least one of these problems at some point in their lives. The goal is to assess whether these symptoms present or get worse as your child's technology use increases.

What Does This Look Like in Real Life?

GAVIN'S STORY: Meme Mistake

Gavin, a typical 13-year-old adolescent, came to our office for an initial consultation, as his mother was concerned about her son's recent irritable moods. She reported that her otherwise easygoing, happy child, was now retreating to his room on a daily basis, had tried to skip school, was talking back and arguing frequently with her and her husband, and now had to be forced to sit at the dinner table and eat with the family on a regular basis. She indicated that she had tried to broach the subject with him but that he'd been stonewalling her with the terse platitude of, "I'm fine."

During the first session, Gavin was unusually quiet and reserved as his mother explained the situation. After his mother stepped away, Gavin eventually opened up that he'd made what he called a "huge mistake." Little progress was made during this first session, although we tried to reassure him that together we could find a solution for his "huge mistake."

In our follow up session, Gavin remained hesitant to share his "huge mistake," but slowly began sharing other information to give us a more complete picture of his life. Near the end of the session, he told us that he liked to repost memes and had become known at his school as the jokester who sent out funny memes. Alas, he had passed along a meme online that he didn't initially understand was racist. Soon kids at school started sharing his post and making derogatory comments, and he was left with the painful realization that the genie was out of the bottle, and that he couldn't undo the damage done. The meme was brought to the school's attention and Gavin was promptly suspended for several days, with the support of his mother. As parents around the school learned of the incident, complaints began flooding the school office that the behavior should not have been tolerated and the punishment was insufficient. Soon enough his family realized he would be continually left out because he was characterized as a troublemaker. This one incident cost him the friends he'd had since kindergarten, as his longtime friends' parents refused to let their children spend time with him on the weekends.

What We Can Learn from Gavin

Gavin's story is not at all uncommon for teens navigating the uncharted waters of today's social media. As with the broader challenge of navigating an emerging social order in real life, today's adolescents are trying to find their own niche online to find love and acceptance among their peers. In Gavin's case, he'd spent his entire childhood with the same group of boys, starting school together, playing sports together, and sharing the experiences of having divorced parents. Gavin understood that he'd made a mistake and felt that his suspension from school was fair, but his expulsion was a *devastating* "social death" that left him rocked to the core of his being, wondering whether he truly was a horrible person who deserved to be expelled. The depressive symptoms that his mother worried over were actually the profound grief over the loss of his peers, the loss of his longtime home in the school community, and the loss of respect from nearly everyone in his extended social network. However, it was the behavioral symptoms that were observed by his mother that prompted Gavin's referral to therapy. Clinically, he certainly had remorse and had learned from his mistakes, and in time started to enjoy coming to therapy to process his choices and make sense of his life going forward. It was just amazingly unfortunate that *one online post* could so radically alter the life of a 13-year-old.

JENNY'S STORY: Girl Gamer

Jenny was a well-liked 11-year-old girl who attended a respected private school along with her two older brothers. With a four-year age gap between her next oldest sibling and her, she was always trying to keep up. After a divorce, her father had primary custody and initiated therapy after Jenny, traditionally an A/B student, came home with a report card full of C's and D's.

Jenny had loved playing on the basketball team and was constantly asking to go on sleepovers with her friends, but since the divorce her mother had shown little interest in their family. Jenny's father worked hard to ensure that she had time with other girls from school, but he felt blindsided when she asked to quit the basketball team, even if her reasons seemed "justified." When Jenny first came to therapy, she presented as a happy, upbeat young tween who was surprised and confused to find herself there. She said that her dad typically let her do what she wanted to and that her grades weren't "that bad."

During her second session, Jenny was an entirely different child. This time around, she told us that she was upset and angry with one of her brothers who'd tattled on her to their father over her gaming habits. When asked why she hadn't mentioned the gaming previously, she said that she didn't consider it to be much of a big deal because all of her friends, and most kids nowadays for that matter, were online with her. She was furious with her father because not only had he taken away all of her games, but he was now making her sit down and go through her schoolwork every night, and also washing the dishes and taking out the trash. We talked about how this sort of thing is quite typical for kids her age, including placing limits on technology use, reviewing homework with parents, and performing chores around the house, and yet she remained livid. After consulting with her father and helping him monitor things more carefully, it became clear that Jenny had not only been gaming after school, but well into the night, and she was even on her phone during school hours. After only a few sessions her A/B grades came back and they settled on her joining the girls' volleyball team with several of her friends. Only then did she fully appreciate just how much gaming had taken over her life in the previous weeks and months.

What We Can Learn from Jenny

It's a *common* misconception today that gaming is exclusively a boys' issue. This case demonstrates not only a typical scenario in which gaming takes over a child's life, but also that it happens to girls as well. Jenny's father was doing the best he could with three kids to support (both emotionally and financially), but he was too trusting of his daughter to keep him informed of her day to day activities. By contrast, his older sons had never needed to be reminded about their schoolwork and both were so engaged in athletics that gaming wasn't ever a priority for them. As parents, we need to remember that our children's behavior is reflective of the culture around them and that they typically will take the path that simultaneously offers them least resistance and the most reward.

Strategies for Managing Your Child's Behavioral Issues with Technology

We don't believe that technology overuse is defined either by a child's desire to use devices, but based upon *how they respond to limits*, and, as they mature, on their ability to regulate their technology use as part of a rich and fulfilling life.

Mismanagement of Time

Technology Use Logs/Screen Time Monitors. Having an intuitive, gut feeling about your child's technology use is not the same thing as seeing actual, quantifiable data. Seeing the raw amount of time that your children spend using particular technology and comparing that screen time with the time they spend playing, sleeping, or at school will give you a full understanding of just how much this can be an issue in your household.

We also strongly recommend that you consider monitoring your own screen time. It can be easy to pass off adult technology use as answering work emails late into the night or touching base with clients in other time zones, but keep in mind that *that's not how your children see it*. If your children see you texting while driving or answering work calls during family time, you'll lose credibility in your ability to enforce rules regarding your children's use of many of those same devices.

After tallying the family's technology use, have a discussion with your children about their use, as they simply may not realize just how much time they're spending on their devices. Interestingly, we've had parents who were shocked by their own use of electronics. Remember, families are holistic units, and this is an opportunity for you to set an example for your children that they'll remember for the rest of their days.

Use Timers. In addition to technology use logs, timers (both the kind built into your devices and good ole fashioned kitchen timers) are an excellent way to compartmentalize technology use. We all know how easy it is to lose track of time when using social media, the Internet, and computers in general. After all, it's quite easy to start researching something online or start online shopping only to discover that 90 minutes have passed without any success. Our kids experience the same scenario, but we all know that they have much less self-control, leaving them even more susceptible to this. Timers will help your kids understand just how quickly time can pass when using technology, and to make sure that their time is spent on other more productive tasks. The earlier and more often you do this with your kids, the more they'll internalize this habit over time.

Although some parental monitoring programs send alerts when the computer is being used and allow you to turn off the device remotely, the goal is to empower your children to monitor their own time. For older children, it provides them with a hard stop for technology use. Blocking software can also allow you to limit your children's access to various websites as well. Be sure to check with manufacturer websites for particulars on any devices your children are spending too much time on.

Changes in School Performance

Follow Your Children's Schoolwork Online. More and more schools today are allowing students and parents to monitor the child's schoolwork online, which offer detailed snapshots of your child's academic performance in real time. By checking in periodically, you can find out when your children miss assignments or perform poorly on tests, and whether or not they're lying to you about those issues. However, we caution against following so closely that you begin to micromanage their academic progress, as this is something that they're going to have to learn with time to do for themselves.

Maintain Contact with Your Child's School. In addition to keeping tabs on your children's academic performance, regular contact with teachers will let them know that you're available if there are problems. Although we don't encourage crossing over into helicopter parenting, it's important to ensure that children and teachers know that everyone is on the same page. Furthermore, following your children's schoolwork and staying in contact with the school will give you a more complete picture of your child's academic life once middle school hits and you have to start teaching your children to advocate for themselves in an academic setting, particularly if they have any sort of struggles with their coursework. This will save all of you the grief of having to deal with a bad report card at the end of the semester.

Use Screen Time as a Reward for Finished Homework. Since your kids will want to play on their devices—but not do their homework—make sure that you dangle screen time as an incentive for them *after* they've finished their homework, with appropriate punishments for missing assignments. Be sure also to focus on your child's *effort* rather than his or her grades, since not everyone is an A+ student. A gifted child can halfheartedly earn B's and C's in classes while a child with average intelligence can pour his or her heart and soul into those same classes and come away with the same overall grades.

Teach Your Kids Organization, Study, and Life Skills. It's never too early to start teaching your kids those *7 Habits of Highly Effective Teens* or *7 Habits of Happy Children*. Human beings are not born knowing how to organize themselves efficiently in the working world, and unfortunately these very necessary life skills are usually not in school curricula. Learning those self-discipline skills is typically an *indirect* byproduct of school—students are judged ultimately by their GPA, regardless of underlying circumstances—but learning those life skills comes in fits and starts, with lots of mistakes along the way, no different from trying to find the right partner or finding the right career. We don't expect our kids to come home from school and know instinctively that they need to devote X number of hours to a particular subject, that they have to study for X exam before a sports competition, or that X standardized test is on the horizon and that they need to start preparing for it. Those things are difficult for college students (and even us adults) to realize, let alone for middle school and high school kids, and that's before we factor in how distracting technology can be for the developing brain.

A good place to start is with a simple Google search of notetaking and study skills. Here you can also work *with* your child's technology to ensure that they prioritize the right things. As your children learn from you and their teachers what your expectations and priorities are, they'll learn to prioritize the things that are most important. Summer school can also be a good resource for study skills classes.

Organize Events for Your Kids. If your kids have gone down the rabbit hole of technology… sometimes you need to flood the rabbit hole. Particularly for younger kids, be sure to organize activities for them *away* from technology. This could include inviting over another parent and child for an outing or taking a group of kids somewhere for fun. Stepping up with creative ways to fill the time for your children away from technology will teach them that there's more to life than looking at screens all day long.

Throw Them Outside. No, we don't mean abandoning your children. But pushing your kids outside for *unstructured* playtime is one of the best things that you can do for them. Structured activities like sports, school extracurriculars, and camps are all important, but so too are the skills that they will learn by filling up time while bored around their neighborhood—using their creativity to come up with things to do with other kids, working through interpersonal problems with other kids, etc. are all things that they'll learn when they're away from their screens.

Tensions with Friends and Family

Take Vacations Without Technology. Disconnecting from technology while exploring a new place, such as the Grand Canyon or Disneyland, can be a great way to bring your family together, without the pressures of day to day life. Yes, we know that a percentage of you are shrieking at the idea of having to spend quality time without the safety net of your devices, but that's precisely the point. Once your kids spend a few days disconnected from the world—but connected with their families—they can relax and connect with everyone in a way that might seem foreign to all of us today. They may even—imagine this—initiate conversations with you. During tech free breaks, because your children aren't on their devices, they won't be subject to the "constant questions" they may normally accuse you of asking. Lastly, keep in mind that "vacations" don't have to be expensive trips to exotic, faraway destinations—they can be as simple as a weekend camping trip or a day at the zoo, but they can create memories that will last a lifetime.

Tech Free Tuesdays. We like to encourage our parents to implement Tech Free Tuesdays (or Wednesdays or Thursdays) which means that after 5 pm all technology is turned off or removed and the family does something together. Obviously this gets harder as older kids go in different directions for school and work, but the important thing is to start young and build healthy habits, while taking into account changing schedules or big school projects.

Shifts in Interests

Help Your Kids Find New Interests. It's perfectly normal for kids to lose interest over time in activities that they previously enjoyed, as they transition from neighborhood games and recreational sports to school teams and school activities. Children who may have enjoyed Legos or playing with dolls when they were very little may be lost (albeit only temporarily) as they try to find a new place in school through activities like sports teams, the school play, the debate team, or designing a section of the yearbook. We all grow and change over time, but we can't use that as an excuse to let our kids spend their days glued to screens. If they don't realize this on their own, require them to find a school activity or a job if they are old enough. If you can find time, we also recommend finding an activity that you both can do, such as volunteering or learning a new skill like meditation.

KEY TAKEAWAYS FROM THIS CHAPTER

- Behavioral symptoms of technology overuse manifest themselves in your child's mismanagement of time, changes in school performance, tensions with friends and family, and shifts in their interests.

- Mismanagement of time includes factors such as an increased demand for screen time, an increase in the amount of time spent on devices, losing track of time, and trying to push back bedtimes.

- Changes in school performance include declines in grades and missing school.

- Tensions with family include increased conflict within the family, spending less time with friends and siblings, and lying and deceiving friends and adults.

- Shifts in interests include a loss of interest in sports and an abandonment of hobbies previously enjoyed, although both may occur naturally as a part of your child's development.

ACTION STEPS

- Oversee your child's time management with technology use logs and timers.

- Verify your child's school performance by checking online and maintaining contact with the school.

- Use screen time as a reward for finishing homework.

- Teach them good life and study skills, organize events for them with friends, and occasionally throw them outside.

- Take family vacations without technology.

- Help your kids find new interests as they grow and change.

FOR FURTHER READING

- *7 Habits of Highly Effective People, 7 Habits of Happy Kids, 7 Habits of Highly Effective Teens* by Steven R. Covey

CHAPTER SEVEN

Managing Physical Symptoms

---

*"A new study claims that poor posture
caused by texting is becoming an epidemic.
I'm not sure if I've been affected, but I have a hunch."*
—SETH MEYERS

THE SECOND AREA WE FOCUS ON IN THE TUC IS YOUR child's physical symptoms. Physical symptoms are often easily overlooked just because we have a tendency to focus on our children's outward behavior rather than their bodies. If your child is having difficulties with technology in the other three areas of health—behavioral, emotional, and interpersonal— then his or her physical health is likely to be affected as well. After entering therapy, many of our parent and child clients have become better observers of these many subtle yet common symptoms of technology overuse.

Signs and Symptoms

Physical changes can be difficult to separate out from the usual ups and downs of childhood and adolescence. Hormones associated with puberty can cause a myriad of physical changes that have nothing to do with technology. For example, your child might develop headaches, require prescription eyeglasses, have disrupted sleep, or become more injury prone while playing sports. At times, pediatricians might warn us that our child is gaining too much weight or is undersized as they grow. Despite all of these natural ebbs and flows that occur as children develop, there are physical symptoms of technology overuse that are similar to the changes described above.

Aches, Pains, and More

Back Issues. Children's bodies are not only *smaller* than adults' but anatomically *different*, and thus the sort of traditional office furniture we typically buy for our home offices and computer rooms isn't built for kids, in terms of both size and design. The combination of time spent in front of screens and improperly designed furniture can leave your kids sitting in awkward positions for extended periods of time and cause the kinds of spine issues and back pain that we otherwise generally don't see in children, in much the same way that your feet would hurt all day long if you wore shoes that weren't the right size for you.

Tech Neck. The 21st century heir to Carpal Tunnel Syndrome and Blackberry Thumb is what medical professionals are calling "Tech Neck" or "Text Neck," meaning that keeping our necks bent at a 45 to 60 degree angle as we stare at our phones for extended periods of time is equivalent to putting a constant 40 to 60 pounds of force on your neck. This is causing the exact same sort of repetitive motion strain as those other infamous long standing issues, and adults who work all day on computers experience similar problems as well. This neck strain is also known to contribute to headaches.

Vision Problems. A wide variety of vision problems can come from the sort of constant strain—this time on the eyes—that comes from working with screens for extended periods of time. Strain on the eye muscles can cause headaches and migraines in both children and adults, while cases of near-sightedness have *dramatically* increased in recent times, no doubt due to all of the time we spend staring at screens. These issues are particularly worse in children because their developing eye muscles are less equipped than those of adults to handle the prolonged physical stress that comes from focusing on a screen for hours at a time. Your children's eye muscles also develop naturally by looking at the horizon, which means that they need lots of play time outside. The prolonged exposure to blue light emitted from electronic devices can also prematurely age the cells in the retina, causing macular degeneration.

Nutritional Concerns

Unusual Weight Gain or Loss. Although weight gain and loss can be part of the usual ups and downs of childhood and adolescence, it can also happen when your children are busy filling themselves with energy drinks and junk food because of the time they spend on their technology. This weight change can also be associated with depression, which can manifest in children by their escaping into their technology. Children will also skip the healthy food you work to give them and instead spend their time snacking on junk food at all hours of the night or eating outside of traditional mealtimes. Three common problems that manifest in the intersection of technology overuse and weight are mindless unhealthy eating while using electronics, using energy drinks to counterbalance a lack of sleep after nights lost playing games, and the corrupting influence of social media posts portraying the "perfect body" leading to girls in particular obsessing over their weight.

Sleep

Dark Circles Under Eyes, Puffy Eyes, or Red Eyes. Dark circles and puffy eyes can occur from a lack of sleep, while red eyes indicate a lack of blinking or lack of sleep while using technology, and also marijuana use in older kids.

Changes in Sleep Habits. With increased technology use, your children may take longer to fall asleep, use their phones as alarm clocks, or wake up in the middle of the night to talk or text on their phones.

Sleep Deprivation/Fatigue. With increased technology use or more frequent awakenings due to cell phone notifications, daytime fatigue can manifest itself both in being tired and in seeming dizzy, both of which indicate a lack of sleep and particularly a lack of *quality* sleep. Another potential symptom is the failure to fall asleep at a reasonable hour. Fatigue can result in irritability, anxiety, dizziness, poor concentration, impulsivity, and even thoughts of suicide. Yes, we have had clients whose excessive fatigue led to depression and thoughts of suicide. *This is a very real issue and should not be taken lightly.*

Cleanliness

Wearing Dirty Clothing. Wearing the same clothes for 5 days in a row might make for a funny movie scene, but it's not funny if your kid is the one doing that. Ignoring their outward appearance or putting off dressing and grooming until the last possible minute is another sign that your kids may be overusing their technology.

Inattention to Grooming. If your child isn't washing his or her hair, doesn't take regular showers or baths, and never trims fingernails, etc. this sort of neglect can be a sign that your children are choosing their technology over cleanliness as well.

What Does This Look Like in Real Life?

PATRICK'S STORY: Left to His Own Devices

Patrick was referred for therapy to help "feel more comfortable with people." A 20 year old male, Patrick had dropped out of school in 10th grade and only recently found gainful employment. As we began his intake, he revealed that his mother had died when he was only 10 years old and that he hadn't ever been able to make peace with her passing. Patrick and his sister were often left home alone as their father took on a second job to pay the bills, even as they all struggled to fill the void left by the loss of his mother. At age 11, Patrick found a "really addicting" video game and told us that within three years of starting the game he was playing *17 hours per day*. Soon his grades collapsed, and everyone suspected that the gaming was the main cause for his dropping out of school. He told us that even by age 12 he spent less time playing with his friends and dropped organized baseball, which until then had been his favorite sport. By age 13, he was so immersed in his gaming that he lost a significant amount of weight, but, fearful of the weight change, he then began running to the pantry between games for the junk food and energy drinks that he could consume in short order while gaming on his computer. Within 18 months, he'd gained 75 pounds and shifted from underweight to obese.

Patrick admitted that his father had tried to intervene and limit his game playing by physically taking away the computer, but Patrick was savvy enough to manipulate his father to get the computer back, exploiting the grief they all felt and his father's inability to fill that hole in their hearts. Patrick's father made threats to send his son to therapy or some other form of treatment to address his gaming addiction, until finally sending Patrick to military school. There Patrick blossomed as a straight A student and was active in extracurricular activities, but was also separated from all of his electronic devices. After graduating in 6 months, Patrick returned home, but soon fell right back into his pattern of playing video games all day long. The weight he'd lost at military school came back and soon he was again sleeping very little. By the time his father ordered him into therapy, Patrick admitted that he felt uncomfortable in the presence of others and wondered aloud if he had a social anxiety disorder. In meeting with us, his goal was to "have more friends."

What We Can Learn from Patrick

Patrick experienced one of the most traumatic events that can happen for a child—the loss of a parent. With that pain and devastation introduced into their lives, along with the void created by their father working all the time, it's understandable that Patrick and his sister were left grieving twice over.

What wasn't good was filling that void with technology, and to such an excess that it taxed his body in devastating ways, despite his placing relatively few physical demands on it . Patrick's excessive use caused him to forget to eat (not at all rare among gamers) and yet in correcting his weight loss he inadvertently swung the pendulum in the opposite direction, while a lack of sleep likely made things even worse.

Patrick's addiction to technology (this definitely crossed the line from overuse to addiction) unraveled what to that point had been a fairly normal childhood—the loss of his mother notwithstanding—filled with friends, sports, and family. Patrick failed to stay connected with his friends, and the video game he turned to contributed to that. In evaluating Patrick , we found that he had never actually had a social anxiety disorder; rather, his social skills were underdeveloped due to his incessant gaming.

MICHELLE'S STORY: Sleepless in Seattle

Michelle was a successful 15 year old high school freshman—a good student, cheerleader, and babysitter. When Michelle turned 13 years old, her parents gave her a cell phone, and they later upgraded her phone plan to include unlimited texting. Her parents turned to therapy when they noticed that she'd developed dark circles under her eyes and regularly drank energy drinks and coffee. They saw that she'd begun skipping meals with the family even when home, was often groggy in the morning, and had difficulty getting out of bed. Michelle dismissed her parents' concerns, telling them that she was tired because she was up late studying, that she wasn't hungry because she ate after school, and that she drank energy drinks and coffee to concentrate on studying.

What concerned Michelle's parents was when they began to notice that she was *never* without her phone and could be found checking it all day long. Michelle carried her phone with her to dinner and into the bathroom, and she slept with it right next to her on her nightstand. When the family cell phone bill arrived and showed that Michelle had sent *6500 text messages* in one month, at all hours of the day, her mother knew it was time to step in. Her parents sat her down and pointed out her texting usage and the signs and symptoms they had been noticing. Despite her protests they began using time management monitoring to limit use at night and made her charge her phone overnight downstairs and out of her bedroom. Her parents saw that their daughter's lack of sleep, poor eating habits, and caffeine consumption could all be traced back to texting all night long with friends.

What We Can Learn from Michelle

Michelle demonstrates several of the signature symptoms of technology over-use, such as energy drinks, caffeine, circles under the eyes, and general lack of sleep. While this may at first seem to be normal teenage behavior nowadays , Michelle's parents were right to step in when they saw her sending 6500 text messages in one month and that she was never without her phone. Forcing her to step back and analyze her relationship with technology before things got worse was a fantastic parenting win for her parents and would allow her to bring her life back into balance going forward.

Strategies for Managing Your Child's Physical Symptoms with Technology

Your children's physical symptoms of technology overuse require creating a healthy environment for them both in terms of when and where their technology is used, but also in *how* it is used. Despite the awkward challenges of childhood and adolescence that can be a normal part of growing up, the physical changes we outline can often signal a *serious* problem and should *not* be overlooked. But they can be managed and mitigated, thankfully.

Aches, Pains, and More

Buy an Ergonomically Correct Computer Station. Be sure that your computer station meets the needs of your children and can adjust as they develop physically. Check the height of the chair and desk to ensure that they meet the ergonomic needs of each of your children and are easily adjustable for everyone who uses that particular setup. This means that the top of the monitor screen should be at or slightly below eye level; the monitor should be no closer than 20 inches from the eyes, or at arm's length; and the keyboard should be in a position that keeps the elbows close to the side of the body and at a 90 degree angle. For kids who like to wiggle around and may not be able to sit still, standing desks also work well, keeping in mind the above ergonomic considerations.

Stretch and Exercise Regularly. Everyone should learn appropriate exercises to counteract the effects of Tech Neck and back problems. Have your children stand up every 20 minutes or walk around and even do necessary exercises that help. Google can be very helpful with finding specific exercises related to these issues. Many middle school and high school gym classes provide instruction on stretching and exercise, so consult with a gym teacher if necessary. We also encourage parents to enroll in weekly exercise classes with their children if technology overuse is an issue. Children benefit because they learn the importance of exercise and you become a good role model for healthy living. Many classes are also offered at a relatively low cost in neighborhood recreation departments and park districts, making them far less expensive and inconvenient than joining a private gym. Other exercise routines worth exploring are the martial arts, meditation, and yoga classes. One family we worked with thoroughly enjoyed a child's yoga book that demonstrated yoga exercises with cartoon pigs… "piggy yoga" as they called it.

Monitor Your Child's Vision. The American Optometric Association (AOA) reports that children are at risk for "Computer Vision Syndrome" if their computer use and other screen time is not well monitored. Computer Vision Syndrome represents a distinct cluster of eye and vision-related problems that arises from prolonged computer use. In addition to the usual eyestrain, symptoms include blurred vision, headaches, dry eyes, and neck and shoulder pain. To minimize your child's risk, the AOA recommends regular eye checkups, limiting time spent sitting at a computer, and taking frequent breaks from staring at a screen. Additionally, the AOA also recommends that the ergonomics of your family's workstation should be adjusted to fit each child properly, to eliminate or reduce screen glare, and to match the lighting levels of the room and computer screen.

THE 20/20/20 RULE

Keep this in mind when using screens for extended periods of time—after 20 minutes, look away at a distance of 20 feet and do so for 20 seconds. Be sure to blink and allow your eyes to rest. Post a reminder note next to your screen or set timers as necessary.

Complete Computer Homework First and Paper Homework Last. Schools today are putting a good deal of your child's homework online and thus it's something that can't be avoided. That said, we suggest having your child do their computer homework first and paper homework later as that will allow their eyes to decompress before bedtime, while also giving the body time to release the melatonin needed for high quality sleep.

Go Find That Blue Light Special. Although shopping at K-Mart is something that may be as foreign to your children as Blockbuster Video and dial-up Internet, the blue light that we've discussed emitted by screens *is* a serious issue as it can interfere with your child's sleep in both duration and quality. Thus we recommend either buying computer glasses for your children that have a blue light filter, or buying a separate blue light filter for the screens they will use, particularly once schoolwork starts to necessitate late night computer use.

Nutritional Concerns

Keep Tabs on Your Cupboards, Pantry, and Refrigerator. Keep tabs on what is being eaten in your household and in what quantities. *Convenience food is not healthy food.* Be mindful of what you are purchasing for your kids and do not buy sodas. While your children are working on homework or surfing the web it is very easy for them to grab whatever "low hanging fruit" they can eat on the fly. Having healthy snacks that are easy for them to eat (string cheese, nuts, fruit, etc.) will set them up for long term healthy snacking habits later in life.

YOU CAN EAT HEALTHY NEARLY ANYWHERE

A common misconception among the general public is that health foods are only found in expensive health food stores. Not so! You can eat healthy at your neighborhood grocery store—generally speaking—by "shopping the perimeter" of the store. The outer perimeter of most traditional grocery stores is home to their stock of fresh fruits, vegetables, salads, milk, fresh juices, the deli, the bakery, etc. while it's the interior aisles that are filled with processed foods in boxes full of preservatives and artificial sugars. Stick to the outer aisles of your store and you'll be fine!

Be Mindful of Where Your Children Eat. Don't let your children eat in their room or while playing games. Kids should only eat at the dining room and in the kitchen, or any other places that the *family* eats. Although obviously we can make exceptions from time to time, limiting *where* your kids can eat will help to limit any mindless eating. Don't allow your kids to use their phones while eating with the family, either, and be sure to model this as well.

Avoid Stimulants... Really. Much like sleep, one important thing to monitor in our children is the use of stimulants, most notably caffeine and sugar. As we all know, caffeine is an ingredient in many of the drinks that our children begin to consume in middle and high school. However, the American Academy of Pediatrics recommends that adolescents (ages 13-18) consume no more than 100mg of caffeine per day (one cup of coffee, one energy drink, or 2-3 sodas) and that children under the age of 13 *should not consume caffeine at all*. Remember, caffeine has *no nutritional value*, acts as a stimulant, and can be mood altering. We believe that children should *not* consume caffeine and hope that you will follow the advice of the medical community on this.

Stimulant use is also of even greater concern for children taking psychotropic stimulant medication for Attention Deficit/Hyperactivity Disorder, such as Ritalin, Adderall, Concerta, Focalin, etc. Children taking these medications should avoid consuming caffeinated beverages entirely as the interaction of caffeine with these medications can cause cardiac problems and panic attacks. See our later chapter on children with unique needs for more information on managing technology for kids with ADHD.

Sleep

Make Sleep a Priority. In today's 24/7 culture, it's a common source of pride to go without sleep, and yet the research tells us that going without sleep is one of the *worst* things we can do for our bodies.

As in the brain research we mentioned in the opening sections of the book, we're finding that *sleep is one of the most important activities that children engage in every day*. While we sleep, the body not only recharges itself but the brain processes information, commits material to long term memory, and performs many of the tasks that it's otherwise unable to complete during our waking hours. Without sleep, our children quickly become irritable, argumentative, and impatient. Healthy physical activities like exercise, sports, and even socializing with friends are still important of course, but those activities all accrue fewer benefits for a child whenever he or she is consistently sleep deprived.

Making sleep a priority is also an important habit for all of us adults, as well. Although corporate America today values the workaholic, and globalization means that it's always business hours somewhere in the world no matter what time it is where you live, plenty of research shows that the longer we work the less productive we are, and that a good night's sleep really, truly does allow us to approach our work every day with a fresh perspective. If your older child is frequently napping it can mean that he or she is not sleeping enough at night.

SO, HOW MUCH SLEEP PER DAY DO WE REALLY NEED?

Newborns 0-3 months: 14-17 hours

Infants 4-11 months: 12-15 hours

Toddlers 1-2 years: 11-14 hours

Preschoolers age 3-5: 10-13 hours

School-aged Children age 6-13: 9-11 hours

Teenagers age 14-17: 8-10 hours

Young Adults age 18-25: 7-9 hours

Mature Adults age 26-64: 7-9 hours

Older Adults age 65+: 7-8 hours

Source: National Sleep Foundation

Keep Your Children to a Consistent Sleep Schedule. One of the best ways to manage your children's sleep is by putting them on a regular sleep schedule, going to bed and rising at the same hours, allowing for weekend flexibility. Over time, this will program their bodies into a regular sleep and wake cycle that will benefit them into adulthood.

Establish Cut-Off Times for Technology Use. We recommend putting away your children's technology at least one hour before bedtime and no later than 10:00pm for adolescents. Using technology immediately prior to bedtime is actually one of the worst things that children can do, as the blue light emitted from screens can interfere with the body's natural sleep cycle and inhibit, by up to 2-4 hours, the release of the melatonin that our bodies need to not only fall asleep to but to have productive, restful sleep.

This is much easier with younger children of course, but if you have teenagers then this will also encourage them to go to bed earlier, since this eliminates a major distraction for them and may incentivize them to go to bed out of sheer boredom. If lack of sleep becomes a significant problem, we recommend cutting off technology as early as 6pm.

No Phones in the Bedroom. Phones in the bedroom are essentially the same as having a television in the bedroom, although it is likely worse for a child. They're simply too enticing for children. Children often cannot regulate their use, so parents must do this for their children. If your kids need to be up at a certain time, use a good old-fashioned alarm clock instead.

Cleanliness

Build Healthy Hygiene Habits. Get your kids in the habit of bathing and grooming themselves every day—bathing, brushing hair, brushing teeth, deodorant, etc. Teach them the importance of presenting themselves well to the world. A good suggestion from one of our favorite parents was to have kids take a bath after school and sports practices, prior to having their allotted screen time.

Teach Your Kids the Importance of Clean Living. While this is an even more difficult challenge for parents than grooming, teaching your kids to wear presentable clothes (not the shirt with the ketchup stain from last night) and to keep their room neat and tidy is an important component of self-worth that is often negatively impacted by technology overuse. In our experience, teaching kids to not bring "street dirt" into their bed is enough to start them down the path of wanting to have a clean, healthy, and sanitary personal space.

DIGITAL DISTRESS

KEY TAKEAWAYS FROM THIS CHAPTER

- Physical symptoms of technology overuse manifest themselves through aches and pains, nutritionals concerns, issues with sleep, and overall personal hygiene.

- Aches and pains include symptoms such as back problems, "tech neck," and vision problems.

- Nutritional issues include unusual gain or loss of weight, poor eating habits, and changes in appetite.

- Problems with sleep include dark circles under the eyes, red eyes, changes in sleep habits, fatigue, and sleep deprivation.

- Personal hygiene issues include wearing dirty clothing for extended periods of time and an inattention to grooming.

ACTION STEPS

- Strategies for aches and pains include buying an ergonomically correct computer station, stretching and exercising regularly, monitoring your child's vision, and completing computer homework before paper homework.

- Nutritional concerns can be addressed by monitoring your food storage areas, being mindful of what your children are eating, and avoiding stimulants..

- For sleep problems, make sleep a priority, keep your children on a consistent sleep schedule, establish cutoff times for technology use, filter out blue light from screens with glasses or screen filters, and keep phones out of the bedroom.

- For cleanliness issues, we recommend building daily healthy hygiene habits every day and teaching your kids the importance of clean living and how to present themselves professionally.

CHAPTER EIGHT

Managing Emotional Symptoms

"You try your hardest to raise your teenagers with patience, honesty and good manners, but they still end up being like you."
—ANONYMOUS

EMOTIONAL HEALTH IS PROBABLY THE MOST DIFFICULT CON-sequence of technology use to measure in our kids, because their device usage takes place against the backdrop of the painful emotional and hormonal roller coaster that we all associate with adolescence, and whose memories are locked vividly in the backs of our own minds for the rest of our lives. As we discussed earlier, teenagers are already brooding and moody simply because of the dramatic changes that their bodies are undergoing, and thus it takes a bit of detective work for us to separate the problems of technology overuse from normal adolescent development, or any other underlying problems our kids might have. Disentangling technology overuse from adolescent development and any other potential illnesses, of course, is key to effective treatment.

Signs and Symptoms

If you're looking over this list and thinking that those symptoms all sound like normal adolescence to one degree or another, we share your frustration. If your children are exhibiting some of the more harmful emotional signs described below, then we recommend seeking help from a professional as soon as possible.

Emotional health factors to look for include:

Sadness. Feeling down is of course part of growing up, and part of the human experience in general. The valleys of sadness that we all experience are what make our peak periods of joy that much more delightful and memorable. In a child, sadness can be triggered by such things as the loss of a friendship, rapid changes in hormones, forced isolation, i.e., global pandemics, or not making the cut for a sports team. That much is normal. But ordinary sadness crosses into depression when it stretches on for an extended period, not seeming to recede with time, combined with a loss of interest in activities that he or she previously enjoyed. This prolonged sadness makes the child more fragile than he or she seemed beforehand, often resulting in tears whenever he or she is disciplined or corrected in ways that previously wouldn't have elicited such a deep reaction. Secondary symptoms of depression to look for in children also include changes in appetite and sleep disruption as well. In our experience, parents are generally very good at detecting this type of depression, so we strongly encourage you to trust your gut with this.

Acting Short-Tempered or Irritable. While depression is often expressed as sadness in children, among older children and adolescents—boys especially—it can instead take the form of irritability and anger. If you get the feeling that you're walking on eggshells around your child and can never say the right thing to calm him or her down, then you should consider that your child may at minimum be experiencing a low level form of depression. In our practice, children who present an irritable depression are described by others as difficult to be around due to their persistent anger and a willingness to turn any discussion into an argument. Depressed children will t̀ way towards everyone around them, and their behavior will oì atmosphere of the entire household.

Feeling Sullen and Withdrawn. Depression can also take the form of dark, withdrawn behavior among children. Children with this form of depression will seem joyless and unemotional towards those around them, and even when everyone around them is smiling and happy, these children will seem somehow emotionless and withdrawn, retreating to their bedrooms to escape the world. Parents should watch for children who continually, repeatedly withdraw from their families and outside activities.

Loss of Interest in Activities or Friends Previously Enjoyed. No matter the form of depression that a child suffers from—sadness, anger, or withdrawal—depressed children over time stop engaging in previously enjoyed activities such as sports, chess club, theater, etc. and fail to remain involved with friends. If they don't completely withdraw from an activity, they might become apathetic about participating in those activities, particularly as you push them to be involved and express surprise at their loss of interest in something that might have previously given them immense pleasure and happiness. This loss of interest can also lead to their leaving homework and other projects incomplete as well. Over time, these children slowly shrink their pool of friends, commenting that they just don't have fun with a particular person or group of friends anymore. They will tell their parents that they're bored with life and will seem unmotivated to fill the chasm emerging in their lives with new interests and activities.

Feeling Suicidal. As we noted at the outset of the book, this is one of the most frightening issues that *any* parent could ever have to deal with in raising a child, and given the dramatic increase in suicides among children (now the second leading cause of death between ages 10-24), this issue simply can't be ignored. *No parent ever* wants to learn that their child is suicidal and given the opportunities that so many of us work to provide for our children, to find that a child is even contemplating taking his or her life can be devastating. It is not a failure on your part as a parent. It is important to remember that even a child who by all outward appearances seems to "have it all" can still feel suicidal, as a child's tumultuous inner life may not always be revealed outwardly, at least in direct, obvious ways. It is all the more difficult to recognize given how much our children live their lives on their devices nowadays and all of the pressures that occupy our time as adults in the modern world.

WARNING SIGNS OF SUICIDE IN CHILDREN

- Talking about wanting to die or to kill themselves
- Looking for a way to kill themselves, like searching online or buying a gun
- Talking about feeling hopeless or having no reason to live
- Talking about feeling trapped or in unbearable pain
- Talking about being a burden to others
- Increasing the use of alcohol or drugs
- Acting anxious or agitated; behaving recklessly
- Sleeping too little or too much
- Withdrawing or isolating themselves
- Showing rage or talking about seeking revenge
- Extreme mood swings

Source: www.SuicidePreventionLifeline.org

A child's suicidal feelings can often come to parents indirectly by way of a concerned friend or from another parent who's learned of your child's situation from their own child. Signs that a child feels suicidal can range from thoughts of "I wish I were dead" or "I would be better off dead" to "I'm going to kill myself on Friday" or "I am going to take these pills after my parents leave the house." *All of these should be taken seriously,* and not merely dismissed as a "cry for help." Given how much more impulsive children are than adults, that means that they're also that much more likely than adults to *act* on that impulse. Much as we all love our kids, they don't have the life experience to understand that whatever their problems and feelings right now—that they might've failed a test in school, that their parents are having problems in their marriage, or that a friend is moving away—that life *will* get better with time.

Children also don't always openly express thoughts of suicide but may indirectly communicate a lack of hope in their future ("I'll never get into college") and see no point in going on with life. Parents should take these comments *seriously* and seek *immediate* psychiatric assistance. And if that care isn't available right away, then *take your child to the emergency room* for an assessment and for their safety. It is *far* better for us as parents to overreact in this sort of situation, as the alternative is incomprehensibly devastating, and something that many parents can never fully recover from.

Engaging in Self-Harm. Nearly 15% of children today report engaging in self-harm behaviors, or behaviors that are done deliberately to harm oneself. For most children, and adults for that matter, self harm is often used as a way of venting painful emotions short of a suicide attempt. But, as we can easily suspect, self-harm incidents can accidentally lead to completed suicides. Self-harm behaviors include self-cutting, taking too much or too little medication (either their own or someone else's medication), hitting or bruising themselves, burning their skin, or suffocating themselves. Evidence of cutting and burning is typically found on the wrists, arms, stomach, thighs, or legs, which is why children who engage in this sort of self-harm will typically wear long sleeves and pants at times when the weather wouldn't warrant that sort of clothing, such as wearing heavy jeans in the middle of summer. These children will also avoid bathing suits and the sorts of activities that would require them to wear (or not wear) clothes that might reveal their injuries.

Debilitating, Irrational Worries. Worries and anxiety, like sadness, are a part of life—it's not a surprise given the stresses of life today that the Australian rejoinder of "No worries" has made its way into the American lexicon.

Our kids will all worry about a recent test score or an upcoming announcement of the varsity soccer roster at school, but some children are simply more prone to worry than other children. To a degree, this is what makes each of us unique, but when children cross into worrying that mom will have a car accident every single time she drives away, or that dad will never return home whenever he leaves the house… this is cause for parents to worry. A child may also obsess over having clean sheets on his or her bed and want to wash those bed sheets every single night, night after night after night. Excessive anxiety and worry can also manifest itself in perfectionism with homework or athletics, and when children inevitably fall short of their own astronomical expectations, that then registers to them as failure. Ironically, this sort of perfectionism can become so debilitating as to be a self-fulfilling prophecy when a child's school performance consequently suffers and their grades decline.

Stomach and GI Issues. Anxiety in children can also manifest in stomach pains and other gastro-intestinal ("GI") issues, ranging from sharp, shooting pains to dull, achy pains. These GI problems can result in either lengthy periods of constipation or frequent bouts of diarrhea, causing children to miss school and requiring frequent visits to the doctor for what is ultimately a psychological issue.

Headaches. Many children experience headaches or migraines during childhood and for some this can mark the beginning of a lifetime of frequent headaches and migraines. Headaches can be the result of dehydration, active participation in activities, stressful school tests, or lack of sleep. However, children who experience significant anxiety and worry will also often complain about tension headaches and migraines.

Explosive Anger, Temper Tantrums, Outbursts, and/or Threats. In our experience, most parents complain about their children's temper tantrums or their adolescent's angry outbursts over the smallest of issues. This is perfectly normal, unfortunately, and is often (whether we like it or not) a rite of passage for teenagers and parents. However, a particular type of anger seems reserved for children who are addicted to either a substance or technology. These children demonstrate *explosive* anger that appears to manifest out of the blue and can leave parents wondering what just happened. This type of anger can result in physical violence towards objects (throwing personal items or punching walls) and towards others in the vicinity.

"The children who need love the most will ask for it
in the most unloving ways possible."
—ADVICE GIVEN TO ROOKIE TEACHERS

Children with explosive anger will make some of their ugliest, most profane and hurtful comments toward loved ones and can even become a threat to the health and safety of those near them. Explosive anger tends to endure for a *lengthy* period of time—more than just a shouting match—and does *not* resolve easily, with something like your child storming out of the room and slamming a bedroom door. A shouting match and slammed doors might make you chuckle if it's an offhand occurrence, but explosive anger leaves *everyone* exhausted, both parent and child alike. Explosive anger will seem scary to everyone and leave family members terrified of what the child might do.

Impulsiveness. By definition, impulsivity—acting or behaving without any forethought or consideration of the consequences—is a hallmark of childhood behavior. As we saw earlier, this is because the area of the brain responsible for problem solving and deliberate planning does not develop later until late adolescence and early adulthood. Younger children are amazing, innocent creatures who blissfully live on the edge without a care in the world, but by later adolescence and early adulthood, they begin to consider and anticipate the consequences of their actions… or so we hope, anyway. However, some children will demonstrate an *increased* impulsivity due to technology overuse. Since video games—and most electronic devices, for that matter—reward impulsivity (one dopamine hit after another as your child hits the reset button on the video game), children can develop either an increase in their overall impulsivity or an increase in their previous level of impulsivity outside their use of electronic devices. This increased impulsivity can become an *incredibly* dangerous combination when mixed with explosive anger or thoughts of suicide.

From Depression and Anger to Cheery Happiness. Children, particularly adolescents stumbling their way through puberty, are typically perceived as moody and emotional, demonstrating unpredictable emotional swings depending on their environment or the people around them. Of course, we parents know that this is very normal (whether we like it or not) and likely the result of changes in hormones, the up and down development of the brain at this stage in life, and the child's inexperience in managing his or her emotions. Parents can become concerned—and rightly so—when their adolescent demonstrates frequent dramatic swings in mood that may even take the child by surprise. A child's behavior can oscillate between depression and intense, angry outbursts over to excitability and happiness in dramatically short increments. These sorts of mood swings may occur unpredictably, and more often than we may expect… or deserve.

Moods Dependent on Technology. Technology-dependent mood states are exactly what they sound like, and many parents in the 21st century are becoming *painfully* familiar with them. If your child's mood improves *only* when he or she is using technology (especially their preferred devices rather than that graphing calculator for advanced math homework) and the child is unhappy, sad, or generally unpleasant away from technology, then their moods are likely to be dependent on the technology specifically. This can make life unbearable for parents and open the door for us to simply leave our children hooked on their devices for the sake of keeping peace around the household.

What Does This Look Like in Real Life?

To help provide some more context with potential technology-related emotional health issues, here are two clinical cases in which technology overuse affected a child's well-being. These cases are very representative of the many patients that come through our door.

JAVON'S STORY: Frequent Flyer

Javon was a fairly typical 15-year-old adolescent boy who was chronically teased at school and on social media that, according to his mom, was due to his delayed onset of puberty, lack of physical coordination, and general awkwardness. She reported that she told Javon to cut off his social media to avoid the bullies from school, but he refused to follow through. His mother stated that she had talked to the school several times about their situation and voiced concerns over his extreme outbursts at home, withdrawing from family time, and getting into fights at school. She was aware that the school counselor had been seeing him on a regular basis and that he was even referred to in unflattering terms by the staff there as a "frequent flyer" for his consistently unruly behavior. The counselor referred them out to private counseling, as Javon's needs were beyond what she could provide for them in a school environment.

Javon came to therapy extremely angry and irritable, telling us that he only agreed to come because his mother had threatened to take away his phone if he didn't attend. He admitted that he hadn't been easy to live with at home and that when angry, he'd occasionally damage the personal property in his room. Through repeated sessions, it became clear that Javon actually met the criteria for depression, which in adolescent boys can manifest more as anger and irritability rather than as a more superficial sadness, withdrawal, or melancholy. Once we were able to start treating him for his depression his mood became *much* more stable and his outbursts dwindled significantly in number.

What We Can Learn From Javon

Typically with adolescent clients, the apparent causes of their emotional outbursts can be deceiving. The most difficult part of trying to work through these issues with school counselors alone is that, as with mental health workers in general, they are often so overburdened with students or clients that they can only focus their time and energy on those in extreme crisis, leaving the rest to fall through the cracks. In some public schools today, for example, it is not unusual for guidance counselors and school psychologists to be responsible for as many as *800 students each*, meaning that falling through the cracks is the norm rather than the exception. In Javon's case, once he was able to work on a weekly basis through the root causes of his emotional outbursts, he made *dramatic* progress. Soon he realized that not only was he having to defend himself within the halls of school, but that at home he was then having to defend himself over social media. On his own volition, Javon began to take breaks from social media and his mood improved, he felt less angry, and he even began to enjoy spending time with his family again.

CAL'S STORY: Separation Despair

Cal, an 8-year-old boy, was brought to therapy by his parents who reported that he had suffered from extreme separation anxiety for the last five years. In the second week of kindergarten, Cal had become apprehensive about going outside for recess to socialize and play with other children. In little time, his apprehension ballooned to extreme anxiety, and he would begin crying and refuse to go outside for recess. In time, Cal began crying to the point of hyperventilating on mornings before school. As the school year continued, Cal's anxiety about school began to surface on Sunday nights and then eventually creeped in on Saturday nights. His parents indicated that they had tried a variety of interventions over the years that had been somewhat successful in reducing his anxiety, but nothing had truly solved the problem. Cal's parents told us that as a young child, he had always been bashful and anxious at birthday parties or when trying new activities, but that he always seemed to warm up to people in time and generally socialized well with others. They agreed that his anxiety had paralyzed the family to the point that everyone now dreaded school days. At a loss for what to do, they brought him in for therapy.

What We Can Learn From Cal

After listening to Cal's story, we encouraged his parents to have Cal take a break from playing video games on his iPad and on the family television set. We informed them that the nervous system of children with anxiety is in a *constant* state of hyperarousal and that it would be important to determine if his technology use was influencing or triggering the hyperarousal that caused him to be so anxious about school. After 30 days, Cal's parents returned for a follow up session and were amazed at the impact that technology had had on their son's anxiety. They reported that after just one week of removing his technology, Cal had only whimpered about school on Sunday night, although he still cried on Monday mornings. After two weeks, Cal no longer mentioned school on Sunday night and by Monday morning he was reduced to a bevy of questions (common in anxious kids) about the upcoming school day. Although his incessant questions could be exasperating, they came as a welcome change for his parents on school mornings. After 3 weeks, Cal's teachers were stunned enough to ask his parents what had changed at home, as Cal was now spending more time outside socializing at recess rather than resisting playing with the other kids. After 30 days, Cal was even able to attend school without any of his previous morning drama. His parents remarked that he continued to demonstrate some anxiety in social situations and at home, but that the intensity had decreased substantially. His story demonstrates how technology can often cause—or increase—underlying anxiety in children.

Strategies for Managing Your Child's Emotional Symptoms

Even though our kids may be "connected" on social media to hundreds if not thousands of "friends," research confirms that today's children are much more anxious, isolated, and lonely than any previous generation on record. There are any number of theories as to why this is the case, and they generally relate to the combination of kids being more overscheduled than ever before, along with the rise of online communication, which has made it difficult for kids to simply be still, decompress, and disconnect from the world. That inability to cope leads them to seek out more electronic connections, which creates a vicious cycle of technology overuse.

A strong relationship between parents and children is one of the most important factors in preventing technology-related emotional issues, and the following activities will help create a positive environment for your children to share their feelings and foster their emotional health.

Have a Family Night Together. If your children are teenagers, you can already hear the groans from them about how lame this would be. Although it can take some convincing at first, having a dedicated family night is one of the best ways to stay connected with your children because before you know it, your children will be headed off to college, trade school, a career, the military, and whatever other opportunities adulthood will provide them. We recommend starting a family night with your children when they are young for just this reason, so that as they grow up it's already an accepted family practice, if not a tradition that they'll remember fondly for years to come.

Structured family time is a great time to become more connected with your children and to provide them with an opportunity to discuss whatever important issues they're facing at the school or in activities, as the immersion in an outside activity will cause them to put their guard down and open up to you. It might take weeks or months for everyone to buy into the concept, but with time and patience, the hope is that soon everyone will look forward to this time together. Family time can be spent in any number of ways, from playing games to spending time outdoors, going to a sporting event or simply enjoying a meal together. Important to remember is that family nights should be technology free... and that includes mom and dad as well.

Have Purposeful Contact Every Day with Your Children. As crazy as life today can be, with everyone enmeshed in hectic, busy schedules, it's important that parents carve out time for a face-to-face connection with their children *every day* if possible. When our kids return home from school and other outside activities, try to establish the practice of spending 5 to 10 minutes decompressing, connecting, and talking with each other. Teach them to find you and touch base whenever they arrive home. The same should also hold true for parents when returning home—go and find your children, talk to them about how their day has gone, and what everyone's plans are for the evening. These informal communications help keep children integrated with everyone else in the larger family unit. And when you're out of town for a business trip, a call home or Skype session can make all the difference.

Consult with a Therapist. Let's face it, parenting is hard and sometimes it *does* take a village to raise a child. If you find that the emotional issues surrounding your child's technology overuse are too overwhelming or unpredictable, don't hesitate to contact a mental health professional—that's what they're there for! Parents can find therapists through their insurance company but in our experience the best recommendations come from other parents who've had a child in therapy and whose experiences we can learn from. If you are friendly with a mental health professional, his or her recommendations and referrals will undoubtedly also be sound as well. Just as you would want a specialist in any other field, it's important to find a therapist with a good reputation for working with children in particular, as one who's good with married couples may not be as effective with children. Even then, a therapist who works well with adolescents may not work as well with young children, and vice versa. Online research can help you narrow down your choices by practice type (family, child, adolescent, etc.) and location. Forums like that of *Psychology Today* also provide lists of recommended therapists in your region. And even if you are turned down by a particular therapist due to insurance problems or inability to take new clients, ask for a referral to a therapist with a good reputation. A good therapist who works well with your child is a priceless resource to have and will make the task of managing your child's developmental issues *significantly* easier.

Meditation. We often encourage children, adolescents, and adults in our clinics to practice meditation. Meditation comes in many forms, e.g., guided imagery, progressive muscle relaxation, or deep breathing, and one form is more likely to be helpful than other forms for any particular individual. We believe that meditation helps people "find their centers" and restore a sense of calmness. Meditation is about being "present" and "in the now," which can assist a child in relieving anxiety or depression. Meditation is not an easy skill to learn; however, the rewards endure for a lifetime. We believe that meditation is so beneficial that children and parents alike should take the time to learn it.

Exercise. If your child is not otherwise involved in athletic endeavors, then we encourage parents to introduce some regular form of exercise. Research is fairly clear that the habit of exercise is beneficial to an individual's overall mental health and can even temporarily relieve feelings of depression and anxiety. Exercise releases endorphins in the brain that have numerous benefits to an individual's overall mental well-being. This is important at all stages of life, and teaching your children to value the role of exercise will assist them in making it a lifelong habit.

Creative Arts. The creative arts can be an outlet for emotional expression for individuals that struggle either to identify their emotions or to express them in a healthy way. The creative arts provide children and adults with a tool to help themselves better manage their emotions. It can be something as simple as buying a coloring or drawing book, or as formal as finding a therapy group dedicated to using art therapy as a means to improve emotional expression.

KEY TAKEAWAYS FROM THIS CHAPTER

- Emotional symptoms of technology overuse include depression—manifested as sadness or acting short-tempered or irritable, feeling sullen and withdrawn, loss of interest in activities and friends previously enjoyed, and feeling suicidal.

- Anxiety symptoms include feeling worried and anxious, stomach and gastro-intestinal issues, and headaches.

- Anger symptoms include an explosive temper, temper tantrums, threats, and impulsiveness.

- Mood symptoms include mood swings from depression/anger to cheery happiness and a child's mood being dependent on the use of technology.

ACTION STEPS

- Have a family night together—Start when they're young.

- Have purposeful contact every day with your children.

- Consult with a therapist if necessary.

CHAPTER NINE

Managing Interpersonal Symptoms

"When my kids become wild and unruly, I use a nice, safe playpen. When they're finished, I climb out."
—ERMA BOMBECK

LAST BUT NOT LEAST, THE FINAL DIMENSION OF TECHNOLOGY use that we address with the TUC is interpersonal relationships.

At face value, it might seem that a child who has hundreds of friends and followers on a social networking site would be popular and connected with people all over the world. Unfortunately, the *opposite* is typically true. One Princeton study found that heavy users of online communications and gaming actually suffered from increased levels of loneliness and depression. Additional research suggests that violent video games might be related to a child's increased aggressive-like interactions with others and a decreased sensitivity towards others' suffering. While research cannot *definitively* conclude that social media and electronic devices are the cause of impaired interpersonal relationships, anecdotally and in the media we know that interpersonal skills are affected by technology overuse and that many of todays' young adults who were addicted to technology in childhood can be flummoxed when confronted with the interpersonal challenges of adulthood.

In clinical settings we're finding that the realm of interpersonal relationships is where technology overuse can have its most detrimental effects in a child's life. These are the difficulties that typically drive our patients into therapy in the first place and on which we spend most of our sessions together navigating the uneven minefields of interpersonal conflict.

Interpersonal skills are an important skill set that we all need to learn in childhood and adolescence, and those skills can deteriorate rapidly in children if they're not given the opportunity to *practice* and *refine* them with others. This is why, for example, play, sports, and group activities in general are so incredibly important for young people—because of the social skills that kids develop through interactions with others in a non-academic setting. Kids learn how to interact, how to process nonverbal cues, how to solve problems both individually and in a group setting, and how to alter their behavior in response to others. This feedback from human, face-to-face communication is the critical factor that distinguishes real world interactions from the artificial world of online interactions, where the lack of secondary, nonverbal cues causes so many of the misunderstandings we have with each other online. Given how as previously noted the brain adapts to its environment over time, the more time our kids spend interacting with technology, the less time their brain spends learning the complex but subtle skills required for successful social interaction. This can make things exceptionally difficult for children later in life, given how important social skills are for real world success today.

Signs and Symptoms

In looking for ways to evaluate whether your child has any issues in forming and maintaining interpersonal relationships, a good place to start is by thinking back to how they managed those relationships before having increased access to their own personal technology. Depending on the age of your child and the opportunities for peer socialization you should be able to gauge whether your child is more of an introvert (someone who draws more energy from time alone, or by spending time with a good book, for example) or an extrovert (someone who draws energy from being out among people). Generally, we as parents should know if our child has had a hard time making friends independent of their technology use, as this typically is no different regardless of environment. Kids generally either struggle or succeed socially in both the online world and the real world, depending on their natural abilities so early in life.

In practice, clinicians typically look to break down a child's challenges in forming relationships by discussing the quality, quantity, and duration of their friendships. Of course, we also know that with the challenges of modern life, it can often be difficult for we parents to maintain our own friendships throughout adulthood (rather than merely contacting friends and former colleagues when we need something) leaving us relatively little time to analyze the development of our children's own social circles. It's undoubtedly difficult, but given how important interpersonal skills are today, let's take a look at some of the challenges that children face with technology use in the development of their interpersonal skills, and how we parents can help guide our children's growth.

Common interpersonal relationship problems

Loneliness. Feeling lonely is a result of being left out or excluded from social groups—or simply believing that we're being left out, whether true or not—and a very painful feeling that all of us have experienced at various points in life. School years are a very challenging time for all of us to find and cultivate meaningful friendships, and exclusion can take many forms—not making a sports team or theater production, not being invited to a party, not sitting at the "right" lunch table, being turned down for a dance or date, etc.—that has become even worse with the introduction of technology, such as when a child is excluded from a group chat or is shamed behind his or her back by classmates or even supposed "friends." Knowing the right app or online game to use or owning the latest device is no different than the experience all of us had in wanting to wear the right clothes, have the right hairstyle, own the right backpacks and accessories, etc. so we could be accepted by our peers.

Focusing on Online "Friends" Rather than Real World Friends. There really isn't any substitute for spending time with peers to teach us how to be kind, how to smooth out conflicts, and how to practice patience when we don't get what we want. Children who shift towards exclusively keeping friends online, to the detriment of friends in real life ("IRL") should raise a red flag. If your child complains about not having anyone to play with in person, or that no one likes them, this is another sign to look out for. Children in this situation often try to manipulate their parents into letting them have more time on devices rather than doing the dirty work of learning how to get out in the world and meet people.

Withdrawal From Family. Technology overuse has a tendency over time to culminate in a child's withdrawing from family life. The pull to remain engaged online with friends, strangers, and fantasy worlds can be so strong that family will seem less and less important, particularly compared to the continual dopamine fix that today's technology can provide. For some children, the hours spent alone in their room playing video games or the late nights on social media artificially satisfy their need for connection with others, but we need to bear in mind that they're really alone. By the time this sort of psychological break from the family unit occurs, a child who overuses technology is likely to have already begun separating from their real life friends as well.

Losing Real Life Friends. Many of the children who overuse technology struggle with maintaining interpersonal relationships, because their technology is so much more alluring than interacting with people in person. As we'll discuss later in *Chapter 13: Children with Unique Needs*, this can also be a case of the chicken and the egg—for example, while children addicted to technology will present symptoms of ADHD, which will then disappear if the technology is taken away. Meanwhile, children with actual ADHD are much more at risk of technology addiction.

Children here, in essence, are unable to disengage from their electronics, even when it costs them friendships. In the increasingly rare instances that they interact in person with their friends from school and the neighborhood, they will tend to discuss *only* their mastery of the video game of the moment or whatever else interests them online. Over time, those friends will tend to disappear simply because they don't share such a narrow interest. If such a child invites a friend over to play, parents will typically find them glued to their technology and have to push the kids out the door to play.

Inability to Read Facial Cues. One sign of a child's underdevelopment of social skills will be the inability to read facial cues from other people. The human face is an amazing creation with so many small muscles and twitches which together communicate our different emotional states to each other—a smile, the raising of an eyebrow, a clenched jaw, etc. Children who spend their days glued to technology will be *much* less proficient in reading these small, minute—but incredibly important—cues from each other, which begets the more general problem below.

General Social Awkwardness. Individuals who feel socially awkward complain that social situations can make them feel anxious or uncomfortable whenever small talk or polite conversation might be required with others. Due to anxiety or nervousness, socially awkward individuals will behave oddly in ways that may inadvertently draw attention to them in unflattering ways. These sort of unsuccessful social interactions can then create a vicious cycle in which the person becomes more nervous around others, which can lead to additional faux pas or ill-received behaviors. Beneath the surface, socially awkward individuals may experience an increased heart rate, shallow breathing, sweating, trembling, and even panic attacks. Given these difficulties, social awkwardness can be paralyzing and lead children who suffer from it to flee to the relative comfort of the electronic devices that don't judge them, and where they can reset a video game or move to a different webpage without anyone looking down on them.

For children who overuse technology for prolonged periods of time, social awkwardness is unfortunately quite common. In these cases, it can stem from a lack of development of social skills or a lack of practice in developing those skills in the first place, often arrested in early adolescence, when children are more likely to drown themselves in technology than face the emerging social complexities of junior high and high school. Generally speaking, the kids who never develop those social skills may be unaware of the feedback they're receiving from peers, while those with an interrupted development of social skills may have some awareness of their deficits.

Poor Communication Skills. Effective communication is important for everyone at every stage in life, and certainly an important part of success in the working world, but here again children who spend their days on technology will lag behind, and the question is whether or not this is something your child innately struggles with or whether it's something gone wrong due to their overuse of technology. Teaching your child to shake hands, look other people in the eye, speak up, be assertive, practice active listening, engage with others, etc. is incredibly important no matter what path they go on to take in their adult lives, and thus you should pay attention to this regardless of their technology use. But deficits here correlate with the other symptoms above as indicative of a child's overuse of technology.

Lack of Empathy. As the saying goes, kindness makes the world go 'round. Empathy is a sign of maturity, and if your child struggles to be kind to others and to understand how other people might see a situation differently, this can be a symptom of low emotional intelligence. The emerging research seems to suggest that the more time children spend on their devices, the less empathetic they become towards others in the real world. If you sense that your child has lost some of the sweetness and kindness that he or she had before being endlessly connected to technology, the technology could be the culprit.

What Does This Look Like in Real Life?

CHUCK'S STORY: Mom Misinterprets Moodiness as Teen Angst

Chuck came to our offices as a quiet, introverted 17-year-old who'd never had a large group of friends. As we completed his intake, he told us that he'd had one close friend with whom he spent much of his time, and that he still enjoyed spending time with both his immediate and extended family. Unfortunately, he and his best friend had a falling out which left him without any close friends to lean on. Chuck began spending more and more time "socializing" in virtual chat rooms and playing online fantasy games. He soon began spending all of his earnings from his summer job to buy characters and other add-ons within the fantasy games, which left him in need of money, which led to his lying to his parents. Soon, they cut him off financially and demanded that he get a year-round part-time job to meet his "expenses," leading Chuck to steal his father's credit card information to make small online purchases that he hoped would fly under the radar.

Chuck's mother received a phone call from school telling her that her son had missed a full week of school without telling anyone. When she confronted him, Chuck claimed that he'd been feeling "ill" and needed to stay home and recuperate. Not believing a word he said, his mother was at first dumbfounded and later on overwhelmed by a wave of "mommy guilt" for having spent significant time away from home that week, barely seeing him at all. She and Chuck's father came to believe that their son was just experiencing routine "senioritis" in school, but in time the truth emerged that he'd spent the entire week playing online games... and to make matters worse, that he wasn't the least bit concerned about school. Chuck began to lose interest in spending any time with his family, and finally his parents had to coax him to even eat dinner with them at home; when they went out for dinner, he barely spoke to them at all.

What Can We Learn from Chuck

Chuck's story demonstrates how an introverted—but otherwise normal—adolescent with good, budding interpersonal skills can regress socially and withdraw from the world once technology overuse takes hold. As technology becomes the center of a child's universe, interpersonal skills can deteriorate. As they disappear into online worlds, the feedback children need for their continued interpersonal growth in the real world becomes almost nonexistent. When situations like Chuck's are allowed to continue, they can *significantly* impair children's ability to build meaningful long-term relationships with others.

SARA'S STORY: Promiscuous Post

Sara, a 17-year-old rising high school senior, was brought in by her mother due to dramatic mood swings. Sara's mom reported that Sara was yelling constantly at her siblings, had been crying over petty little things, and more recently had started screaming that she would be better off dead. Sara's mother became terrified and immediately sought out professional help. She'd initially believed that Sara's dramatic mood swings were due to the usual challenges of puberty and would pass with time, but Sara's more recent remarks about death made her mother believe that this was something to be truly worried about. During our initial session, Sara characterized her mother as overprotective and stupid and said there wasn't anything wrong with her and that she couldn't wait until she was off to college.

Over the course of three sessions, Sara opened up to us about her romantic relationships. She stated that she'd had her first serious boyfriend when she was 15 years old and that while they'd never had sex together, the two of them had still sent nude images and videos back and forth to each other. After dating for six months, she broke up with him and later became interested in one of his friends. Sara revealed that her now ex-boyfriend had retaliated against her by sending her old naked pictures to all of his friends. Soon, every day at school her ex-boyfriend's friends and even other kids openly teased her for being a "slut." Sara was relieved that this had at least happened at the end of her sophomore year, as that gave everyone the summer to forget about the incident, even as it hurt her deeply. In telling us her story, Sara tearfully revealed that she'd felt "so stupid" for sending those images in the first place and was ashamed that everyone in her school community knew what she looked like naked and was probably still mocking her behind her back. She vowed firmly that she would never ever again date anyone from her school to avoid that kind of shame and embarrassment.

In a later session, Sara disclosed that six months ago, she'd met a young man online and had developed a relationship with him. He'd been quite complimentary of her, calling her "baby" and telling her she was "hot." He told her he eventually wanted to meet in person, but didn't have the money at the time to make the trip. In time, after making repeated requests to visit her, he asked her if she would be willing to have cybersex and masturbate with him online until they could meet. Sara told him that she felt uncomfortable with the idea but, not wanting to lose him, reluctantly agreed. Not surprisingly, immediately after she "performed" for him on her webcam, he let her know that he had recorded the video in its entirety so he could always have her with him. She immediately regretted her decision but was resigned to the idea that there wasn't anything she could do about it. The following day, when she refused to perform a different sex act in front of the webcam for her "boyfriend," he blackmailed her into performing once again with the threat of sharing her videos "all over the Internet." Sara was devastated that such a thing could happen… again.

What We Can Learn from Sara

Sara's story is tragic, and not at all uncommon, given the number of girls who've walked through our doors completely destroyed by looking for love online after a bad relationship with a high school peer. Sara felt an incredible sense of shame and believed she was "so stupid" for being manipulated into performing online again for a boy. Sara was also deeply hurt by the violation of her trust from someone she loved, who'd tricked her into doing something illegal and that could have disastrous emotional and lifelong consequences. The anger and mood swings she released at home had been triggered by her poor self-esteem from having this happen to her—not once but twice—in her life. She was losing faith in her ability to distinguish between good and bad people, and she continues to struggle with interpersonal relationships.

Strategies for Managing Your Child's Interpersonal Relationships

These strategies are key to helping your children who have either lost or failed to develop important social skills due to the isolation that's so typical of technology overuse. Learning, developing, and refining these skills are critical aspects to ensure that your children are centered primarily on the reality around them rather than the artificial world of technology.

Model Good Communications Skills with Your Children. One of the best ways to build good communications skills in children is to spend time with them, showing them what healthy face to face interaction looks like. Our children are *always* watching us and if we lose our cool over every little inconvenience we encounter, then our kids will undoubtedly default to that same behavior when they become frustrated. Kids will absorb how you speak to others and carry yourself, or the ways in which you interact with friends, work colleagues, the postal carrier, the wait staff at a restaurant, or strangers on the street.

Meet Your Children Halfway. If you're a parent of teens, for example, one of the best ways that we've found to communicate with them is through text. That's not to say that we should text our children to come down for dinner, or as a replacement for important heart-to-heart conversation, but that sending our kids an occasional message during the day to check on how they're doing lets them know that despite the generation gap, their parents aren't "stuck in the Dark Ages." This keeps the lines of communication open—on their terms, somewhat—and lets them know that you're willing to work with them as the world continues to evolve. Our clients have consistently found that this technique is particularly positive, as both children *and parents* feel happier and more connected to each other. And it works wonders with grandparents as well too.

Try the "Open Texting" Experiment. This is a strategy that may make your children want to disown you, but it is one of the best and most effective ways of teaching them about electronic communications, so we believe it's worth the fight.

Find a large writing surface (a large piece of cardboard or poster board, a chalkboard, a whiteboard, etc.) and secure it on a wall in a public area of your house. Next, find one of your child's old text conversations and tell them that the two of you are going to publicly recreate the conversation, one comment after another. Be sure to promise your child that you will not judge or criticize what is written on the texts—profanity, sexually charged words, etc.

Have your child write down their texts in one color of construction paper while you write down their friend's texts in another color. Then, one by one, place the comments up on the writing surface in the order that the conversation developed. *Be sure to choose a text conversation your child had that included inappropriate language or other comments you don't believe your child would've made in person.*

After taping the texts to the surface, take time with your child to pause and reflect on the conversation. Ask your child if the conversation would have been the same if it had taken place face-to-face and if they would want to change any of the comments they'd made. After your child offers his or her thoughts, take the time to provide your own constructive feedback about the conversation. *Be sure to point out the other person's perspective* and whatever other issues you feel are important. It is vital throughout the exercise that you *do not become judgmental* and keep an open mind. Remember that we were all adolescents once and talked in ways that would've disappointed our parents. The difference is that today's "private" conversations are broadcast over text, Tweets, and other instant message services that become public... and permanent. Use this exercise to help your child to develop their interpersonal skills and to understand the emotional impact that our words can have on others.

To encourage your child to participate in this activity, offer to share some of your own text conversations. In fact, recreating an electronic argument between you and your child may be a fantastic way to discuss interpersonal skills—what you should or should not have said, what you meant to say, how things can be perceived, etc. If your child absolutely refuses to participate in this exercise, then take the opportunity to discuss the fact that *all* texts are in the public domain and can be mined by others today. A child's refusal to participate in this activity can also serve as an excellent catalyst for this sort of discussion about the law of unintended consequences.

Find a Social Skills Group. For some children who demonstrate significant social awkwardness or simply poor social skills, a social skills group dedicated to educating kids and providing them with opportunities to safely and comfortably learn and practice new social skills is a great option that can dramatically decrease social awkwardness or anxiety in children who overuse technology.

Empowering Empathy. Empathy can easily be modeled for our children. In fact, it is the everyday "little things" that parents do in life for others that serve as a model for children to learn how to "pay it forward." The care packages we give them when they head off to camp or the fun notes they find in their lunch boxes teach them how to care for others in small but meaningful ways. Discussing events around the world and how those events affect other people, at a level that's developmentally appropriate, helps them to understand the perspective taking that's the foundation of empathy.

Give Your Children the Gift of Time. The gift of time for your children is one of the most important gifts you can give them. Whether we struggle with working multiple jobs, paying the bills, or just being exhausted by everything occurring in life, we must find moments in our days and time on the weekends to interact with our children. We've mentioned finding family time repeatedly throughout this section simply because we've discovered in our patients that family time was often quite lacking in their lives. Don't freak out if you realize that perhaps you are not spending enough quality time with your children; you can always make changes… and there is no better time than the "present."

Have Your Kids Join Team Activities. Lastly, group activities provide children with the opportunity to build communication and social skills. We don't care if the group is associated with sports, creative arts, religion, school, or other recreational activity, the point is that children need to interact with other children to first develop and then later hone their social skills. The feedback from others, whether children or adults, assists the child's brain in pruning the region of the brain responsible for social interaction. The practice they receive is instrumental in moving the pruning process forward. And they just might make a friend or two along the way!

KEY TAKEAWAYS FROM THIS CHAPTER

- Interpersonal symptoms of technology overuse include alienation–loneliness, focusing on online friends rather than real world friends, withdrawal from family, and losing real life friends.

- Other key symptoms to look for include poor emotional intelligence, social awkwardness, poor communication skills, and a lack of empathy.

ACTION STEPS

- Use technology to your advantage and use the social platforms they do.

- Meet your children halfway, text with them or play videogames with them.

- Try an open texting experiment to help teach your kids the difference between private vs public and how to protect your digital reputation.

- Find a social skills group if your child's skills have fallen behind his or her peers.

FOR FURTHER READING

- *Emotional Intelligence: Why It Can Matter More Than IQ*, by Daniel Goleman

- *How To Win Friends and Influence People*, by Dale Carnegie

SECTION THREE
Facing Today's Challenges

CHAPTER TEN

Video Games

"I like video games, but they're really violent.
I'd like to play a video game where you help the people
who were shot in all the other games.
It'd be called Really Busy Hospital."
—DEMETRI MARTIN

ONE OF THE MOST DRAMATIC ILLUSTRATIONS OF HOW FAR technology has advanced in our lifetimes is in the absolutely stunning, lifelike images of today's video games, particularly when viewed on a large, high definition television screen. The complex worlds and character journeys of today's games are more than a few light years ahead of the pixelated blobs that we first saw in the 1970s, manipulating simple one button joysticks in front of heavy old television sets with primitive versions of Pac-Man and Donkey Kong, and the radical improvements brought later on by Nintendo and Sega.

Of course, what's fun and enticing for a kid can be more than a little disconcerting for a parent. An infamous game like Mortal Kombat, in which players don't merely kill their opponents but finish them off with gruesome "fatalities" like ripping their opponent's head off (with the spinal cord dangling below, no less) or watching their opponent thrown off a cliff (only to be impaled by a large spike below) might seem fun to young boys… but we parents tend to have a slightly different reaction. Controversies have also arisen with games like the Grand Theft Auto series featuring prostitutes, drug dealers, and ever more bloody, realistic depictions of violence. You work hard and do your homework to find a nice place to live in a quiet neighborhood with good schools nearby, only to have these less than savory elements of society brought right back to your children through their video games. The irony isn't lost on us, either.

Answering the Call of Duty… Will Take More Than a Fortnite

As with smartphones, a pall of dread rolls across the suburbs of America whenever a new video game comes out. Soon, our children join every other child in telling parents that the game isn't too expensive, that everyone else is buying it, that it only has a certain rating on it, that every other kid has parents who "get it," and after being fed, clothed, and sent to good schools, our kids tell us through fits of tears and temper tantrums that we're horrible parents and that we don't love them. Although a good percentage of games *are* age appropriate and without questionable content, those aren't the ones that make the news, nor are they necessarily the ones that sell millions and millions of units. There's a lot at stake when your kids ask to play popular games with all sorts of violent content. And if you've seen the video games that have been released to the public, just imagine the games that *haven't* been released.

Video gaming today is a huge, influential industry. Consider, for example:

CONSUMER SPENDING ON VIDEO GAMES WAS $36 BILLION IN 2017

- 64% of U.S. households own a video game device; 60% play daily
- 45% of game players are female
- 72% of parents limit their child's time playing video games
- Asia accounts for more than half of the global gaming market today

Source: Entertainment Software Association

Video games today are one of the most popular forms of entertainment, displacing many of the traditional sectors of film, television, and music. Much of this is generational and promises to accelerate with time.

The Bonus Levels of Gaming

Before we disparage *all* video games, it's important to note that the video game industry does have plenty to be proud of, not only as a fun leisure activity and growing economic colossus but also in the skills that games can teach children. There is research that supports the claim that moderate playing can increase hand-eye coordination, problem solving, strategic thinking, pattern recognition, and concentration; moreover, gaming also provides skills that traditional board games like checkers, chess, and backgammon have taught children for generations. In a historical context, video games are just the latest in a tradition of gaming that stretches back to parchment games in ancient Babylon, and promises to continue its wholesale transition to virtual and augmented reality games sooner than we think.

It's important to remember that today's video games don't just include bloody first-person shooter games but also games like Solitaire or Flight Simulator, as well as strategy-heavy fantasy games like the Civilization series, all of which do an excellent job of teaching higher level thinking skills to kids in a fun and socially engaging way. As with the best classroom teaching, your kids don't even realize that they're learning—and that's a long way from the kind of rote, puritanical model that defined education for centuries, with the memorization of multiplication tables and diagramming of sentences, for example.

The Mindcraft of Minecraft

The problem with video games today, from an addiction perspective, is that they overload the same neurological pathways in the brain that every other substance or process addiction does, and they can leave children at risk for other addictions later in life. Research tells us that video games act on our dopamine pathways by creating a demand loop for the pleasurable behavior, while the release of norepinephrine leaves players feeling a heightened response, and serotonin levels are then affected by virtue of kids not getting enough sleep and gaming too much.

This causes the same problems of gray and white matter degradation along with the thinning of the cerebral cortex that we discussed earlier. Likewise, as with heroin or cigarettes, it's easy to pick up this addiction after years away from it just due to the priming of the brain that takes place from years of repeated use in childhood and adolescence.

The Moral Kombat of Violent Games

One of the most prominent criticisms of video games—but most especially *violent* video games—is that they desensitize kids to violence. The blood and gore that was once limited to battlefields or the occasional war movie is now available for children to immerse themselves in over and over again, such that chasing after bad guys with a machine gun, a pick axe, or a chainsaw no longer seems as foreign and shocking as it once was, or probably should be.

Research thus far does not point to a *causal* link between video games and violent behavior, although this is a classic chicken and egg scenario—do the video games cause children to become violent, or are alienated children (those already prone to violence) more likely to play violent video games in the first place? This is the frontier of research right now, and generating good science around it is a challenge. Regardless, there *is* clear and abundant research about violent video games' reducing empathy and increasing aggression among players, consequences that can serve as precursors to violence.

One additional issue with violent video games is that even if they're designed to feel cartoonish, and even if players see a reduced amount of blood, the *goals* of the games typically still entail violent means and ends—measuring success in the number of kills, shots to the head, etc. along with smug jokes about soliciting prostitutes and putting them in car trunks. Research has yet to examine the full effect of immersion in this sort of mentality as entertainment, but at the very least, we find it more than a bit disturbing to train children to laugh at the pain and suffering of people at the margins of society—even fictional ones.

Some Cheat Codes for Managing Your Children's Use of Video Games

" 'When I grow up, I want to marry a grown man
addicted to playing video games,' said no woman ever."
—E-CARDS ONLINE

Be an Informed Consumer. In response to consumer pressure, the video game industry introduced its own ratings system a generation ago, which we *highly* recommend parents refer to. As with films and television, video games are reviewed before their commercial release, because a game that sells 100,000 units under a restrictive rating is better than a game with a false rating that ends up being pulled from store shelves. And, just as with films and television, you can expect that your kids are going to be in a rush to see the latest, most gory game possible, to keep up with their friends.

VIDEO GAME RATING CATEGORIES:

Everyone (E); 34% of games: Content is generally suitable for all ages. May contain minimal cartoon, fantasy or mild violence and/or infrequent use of mild language.

Everyone 10+ (E-10); 22% of games: Content is generally suitable for ages 10 and up May contain more cartoon, fantasy or mild violence, mild language and/or minimally suggestive themes.

Teen (T); 31% of games: Content is generally suitable for ages 13 and up. May contain violence, suggestive themes, crude humor, minimal blood, simulated gambling and/or infrequent use of strong language.

Mature (M); 13% of games: Content is generally suitable for ages 17 and up. May contain intense violence, blood and gore, sexual content and/or strong language.

Adults Only (AO); percentage not reported: content suitable only for adults ages 18 and up. May include prolonged scenes of intense violence, graphic sexual content and/or gambling with real currency.

Rating Pending (RP): Not yet assigned a final ESRB rating.

Sources: Entertainment Software Rating Board,
Entertainment Software Association

Know Your Kids. While this is obviously good general advice for any parent, in this case we mean that you should understand your children and their sensitivities. While some kids can play the most mindlessly violent video games for hours on end, some more sensitive kids are put off by the blood, guts, and gore, and can develop nightmares from even limited exposure to such games. This is especially a concern when you have older and younger children in the same house, as your older kids won't want to play games geared towards younger children, and your younger children may not be emotionally mature enough to handle the subject matter of games designed for older kids.

Steer Your Kids to Games with an Educational Angle. While we're not the type to say that fun isn't allowed, not all video games are created equal. Today, many parenting magazines offer reviews of the latest video games your children may be craving. Whenever birthdays or holidays are approaching, we recommend spending a few minutes online researching which ones would be best for your children, depending upon, depending upon their developmental stage. For example, a child in need of more exercise might benefit from a game that includes strenuous physical activity, like Wii Sports Resort, while a child whose fine motor development is lagging might benefit from playing a game that requires dexterity, like Guitar Hero. A child struggling with math skills might benefit from a gambling game that requires them to add and subtract constantly. A more precocious child might benefit from playing a trivia game like Jeopardy or You Don't Know Jack, etc.

Finding the right video games can be a great way as a parent to kill two birds with one stone. Not only will you be able to help your child overcome any developmental issues he or she may be having—in a way that's much more fun than physical therapy or after school tutoring—but also you'll be providing something to cling on to and develop as a healthy interest, rather than the latest mindless shooter game.

Keep Your Video Game System Under Lock and Key to Control Access. If your household has a traditional video game system, we *strongly* recommend keeping the system under lock and key so that the adults control access. As with their phones, kids will play video games for all hours if left unattended. Today's video game systems are now implementing parental controls, and we recommend using these as a first option if you don't have a locking credenza or entertainment center. Another way to control access to your kids' video game systems is to keep something like the controllers or power cable separate and only hand them over to your children for certain periods of time.

PARENT CONTROLS FOR COMMON VIDEO GAME SYSTEMS

XBox: XBox uses two sets of parental controls—through the device itself and then through your online accounts. On the device, under the "settings" menu is a family menu in which you can change the settings for each of your children's accounts. And in your XBox account, under the "security" menu, you can block or allow individual programs for each child, along with customizable settings for various programs.

Playstation: First, make sure that the "firmware" (the basic operating code that operates the machine) is updated. Have each of your children create an individual account, which will include entering a birthdate, so the software knows how old your children are when playing. This will allow you to manage which features (Blu-Ray, Internet browser, etc.) are allowed and which particular game ratings your children can play. Newer versions of Playstation firmware also allow you to limit the amount of time and the hours during the day that your children can play games.

Nintendo: Newer Nintendo consoles allow parents to monitor usage with an app called Parental Controls, available for both iOS and Android. Beyond the controls built into the console itself, the app allows parents to block particular games for their children and to restrict the amount of time that kids spend playing games every day. Nintendo also allows parents to restrict in-game texting and posts to social media. Likewise, the Parental Controls free smart device app can link with the Nintendo Switch to easily monitor what and how your children are playing.

No Video Games Until The Homework Is Done. Although your kids will hate you for this, it's an important principle to establish *early* with your children—that video games are a reward, but that *school comes first*. This is the time management equivalent to eating your vegetables before having dessert, and few things are more difficult for parents than to have to force their children to put away the video games and do their homework.

Include Video Game Use in Behavior Contracts. This is one of the best carrot-and-stick ways to incentivize your kids to behave better. If your children are having problems in school or you need them to contribute more around the house, then allowing them a certain amount of time to play video games, or agreeing to purchase a certain video game, is an excellent incentive to steer your children's behavior. Keep in mind also that if your child is begging for a brand new video game, *you don't have to buy it right away*.

Keep Televisions Out of Your Kids' Bedrooms. As a companion to regulating your kids' use of video games, we *strongly* recommend keeping television sets out of their bedrooms as well. Although not as awkward, cumbersome, or costly as the TV sets you grew up with, a fancy flat panel television set in the bedroom is an invitation for your children to isolate themselves and also gives you less control over what your children watch, particularly if (or once) they get around the parental controls.

Turn Off In-App Purchases and Keep Your Credit Card Info Under Wraps.
For games on phones and tablets, the initial purchase may be free, but from
there many games and apps offer all sorts of add-on purchases of extra
players, cheat codes, etc. This is how you get that surprise $3,000 bill from
your credit card company and your child is grounded into middle age. We
recommend turning off in-app purchases for the device your children use,
although newer devices are now adding an "ask permission to buy" that will
allow you to approve the purchases that your children want or need, on a
case by case basis. This solves the problem of purchasing apps that they'll
need for school.

Play a Game or Two with Your Kids Now and Then. This is a great way to
connect with your kids today and to understand the world they live in. Not
only will you get a chance to spend some quality time with them, but while
your kids are enmeshed in whatever game you're playing, *they'll have their
guard down.* If there's something that you want to talk with your children
about, doing so while they're busy running up the score on you in Guitar
Hero, slamming the ball back at you in a tennis game, or chopping your head
off in the latest zombie game is one of the best times to do so.

And for the Particularly Addictive Games, and Your Younger Kids… For
younger kids, we recommend first setting a hard cutoff time like 7 or 8pm
and then letting them finish one more game. This gives them the sense of
playing longer and not having to leave mid-game, yet the end time continues
to be under your control. Younger children naturally have more difficulty
controlling their feelings of frustration, and competitive, addictive games
can push your young children's frustration tolerance beyond their control.
We recommend that you keep your younger children near you when they
play games, so you can intervene if they begin to lose control. Another way
to control or limit their frustration is to have the audio play through the
television, as this permits you to monitor all the game players and intervene
again if the competition gets out of control. Finally, we encourage all families
to have at least one parent learn the games their youngest children are playing. This can also be a great opportunity for some sibling bonding between

older and younger children, too. Kids *love* the opportunity to teach their parents and older siblings how to do something, and they will revel in being more skilled than you.

KEY TAKEAWAYS FROM THIS CHAPTER

- Video gaming is a $36 billion industry that is growing rapidly worldwide.

- Many games do teach kids valuable critical thinking skills.

- Although violent games have been shown to increase aggression and reduce empathy, to date there isn't a proven *causal* link between video games and violent behavior.

- Parental controls have improved dramatically but vary from device to device.

ACTION STEPS

- Do your homework on whatever games your children want you to buy.

- Know your kids' sensitivities before you allow a particular game in your house.

- Control access by locking up gaming consoles and using parental controls.

- Never let your kids play games until their homework/chores are done.

- Keep television sets/streaming devices out of your kids' bedrooms.

- Turn off in-app purchases, and never give out your credit card info.

- Play a game or two with your kids from time to time.

FOR FURTHER READING

- *Grand Theft Childhood: The Surprising Truth about Violent Video Games and What Parents Can Do*, by Dr. Lawrence Kutner and Dr. Cheryl Olson

- *Playing Smarter in a Digital World: A Guide to Choosing and Using Popular Video Games and Apps to Improve Executive Functioning in Children and Teens*, by Dr. Randy Kulman

CHAPTER ELEVEN

Pornography

"The Internet was created by the U.S. Defense Department
as a decentralized, fault-tolerant network to ensure that
in the event of a nuclear war, American soldiers would have
continued access to pornography."
—INTERNET JOKE

A Long Way From Dad's Old Playboys

For a few generations of teenage boys, it was a rite of passage to stumble upon their fathers' hidden, dusty old collections of Playboy magazines to unlock the secrets of female anatomy. But times have changed ever so slightly in recent decades. The magazine that once sold 5.6 million copies a month in the 1970s had an identity crisis in the 2010s, briefly removed nudity from its magazine, later reduced its publishing schedule to quarterly, and announced in early 2020 that the Spring issue will be its final print issue of the year, if not ever. You can take it as an article of faith that today people might actually be reading Playboy magazine (online) for the articles as, otherwise, this icon of the sexual revolution is struggling to compete in an industry that, for all intents and purposes, it invented. With interactive sex simulations available online for today's adolescent boys, the

149

airbrushed still photographs of nude models in a print magazine are down-right tame.

Dirty pictures have undoubtedly been around in some form or another since the dawn of civilization, but pornography today took its (relatively) modern form in the 1600s, defined by a violation of social taboos and the intent to sexually arouse consumers. What's truly shocking about the contemporary pornography industry though is the unprecedented *size* of it:

- Porn is now a *$100 billion* global industry, with $12 billion from the U.S. alone

- Traditional Hollywood companies release 600 films a year for $10 billion in profit; porn companies release 13,000 films a year for $15 billion in profit

- 35% of all Internet downloads are porn-related

- The world's largest free porn site received *33.5 billion* site visits in 2018 alone

- 64% of all young people ages 13-24 look at porn once a week or more

- Children under 10 now account for 22% of porn consumption under age 18

Sources: FightTheNewDrug.org, Medium.com, Enough.org

The porn industry has also, ironically enough, been at the forefront of America's technological innovations over the last 50 years as well. While we aren't going to address any of their more "commercial" inventions in a parenting book, it was the porn industry that first capitalized on the independent film possibilities with the famous 1970's film *Deep Throat*. The porn industry moved out of seedy neighborhood movie theaters and into American homes in the 1980s through the use of VCRs and later in the 1990s was at the forefront of Internet content. Porn companies then tipped the scales in the choice of the home video industry to adopt Blu-Ray over the HD DVD format, and are now pioneering virtual reality work as well. No wonder Hugh Hefner's magazine is on life support.

While we'd all like to believe that our kids are the sweet and innocent ones who will somehow avoid exposure to this online material, common sense says otherwise. The old excuse used by males of every age that they only read Playboy "for the articles" doesn't quite hold water with porn sites, either.

Today's pornography, in addition to the sheer volume of it, can cater to every possible niche imaginable, along with more than a few that you never imagined and probably don't want to imagine. Beyond the reflexive shock of, "Wow, I didn't know that anyone was into that sort of thing," the vast array of pornography available online today has plenty of truly violent, shocking content featuring individuals held against their will, rape and rape fantasies, asphyxiation, and, worst of all, child pornography, alongside vanilla mainstream pornography of the sort that Playboy pioneered.

ONE MESSAGE WE NEED TO MAKE CLEAR TO ALL OF OUR READERS:

POSSESSION OF CHILD PORNOGRAPHY IS A **STATE** AND **FEDERAL CRIME** AND SHOULD BE TREATED AS SUCH. IF YOU OR YOUR CHILD COME INTO POSSESSION OF ANY SORT OF CHILD PORNOGRAPHY, DELETE THE IMAGE IMMEDIATELY.

In our work with law enforcement, we're continually horrified by the sheer amount of child pornography available today, and given the fractured, parochial mandates of individual jurisdictions that stand in sharp contrast to the global reach of the Internet, by how difficult it is for law enforcement to shut down child pornography. In effect, the battle against online criminality amounts to one continuous global game of "whack a mole," with law enforcement chasing criminals across every corner of the globe—whenever a site is taken down in one jurisdiction, it magically reappears almost overnight somewhere else in the world, requiring a whole new set of coordination and cooperation between jurisdictions. As with hate groups, terrorist cells, or even your local bowling league, the Internet allows people with shared interests to find each other, and nowadays that includes pedophiles. And as with violent video games, if you've seen the porn that makes the news, you *really, truly* don't want to imagine the material that *doesn't* make the news. Nor do you want to know the material that bounces around worldwide on the dark web, never to truly be deleted.

So Why Is This a Big Deal Now? Pornography has been Around for Years!

A common reaction today is to dismiss pornography as not being much of a big deal. Sexually explicit material is nothing new of course, but what *is* new is how incredibly *accessible* it is.

Most big cities in history have probably had some sort of red light district where its citizens could seek out whatever particular vices they craved, sexual or otherwise. In previous decades, that meant pornographic movie theaters and bookstores of the sort that filled Times Square and Hollywood in the 1970s, with plenty of magazines and videos to buy, or the speakeasies of 1920s and 1930s organized crime that catered to Americans' pent up demand for alcohol. Unfortunately, today's vices aren't merely confined to one particular area of town, and you don't have to know the secret knock on the hidden door in the back of a hotel to get in—they're accessible on just about every digital device you own, and which your children own. That's removed much of the social stigma long associated with this sort of behavior, and the personal shame that came from seeking it out in those seedy neighborhoods as well.

Today, children on average are first being exposed to online porn *at 8 years of age*—this typically coincides with the time your children first start doing research for school reports—and begin chronic viewing at age 11. The porn industry knows this, which is why, as with the tobacco industry beforehand, they're going where their future consumers are, in subtle and insidious ways.

The ubiquity of this material makes it that much more difficult for you as a parent, of course, which is why it's worthy of its own chapter in a book on raising children in the digital age. Pornography is simply everywhere today, which makes it that much more difficult for parents to teach children healthy attitudes towards sex and sexuality while a global industry inundates your children with images they aren't mature enough to understand.

The second concern beyond the sheer volume of pornography available today is the many new formats in which it's being sold and presented to the public. As we noted above, for better and for worse, the adult entertainment industry is typically at the forefront of creating new multimedia content. Today that includes not merely traditional filmmaking (*Deep Throat*) or still photography (Playboy) but interactive 3D content which gives the viewer the simulation of engaging in sex with a virtual partner, "Choose Your Own Adventure"-style interactive content, webcams, striptease, sexual chat rooms, and more interactive media to come. If the content weren't so salacious, we might all marvel at the technical sophistication in the work they're doing.

How Pornography Corrupts Children's Development

"Pornography has many, many different effects, but the central one that exists regardless of age at its base, pornography commodifies the sexual act. [Pornography] turns something that is intimate, human communication and intimate connection with another human being into something which can be bought and sold."
—DR. MICHAEL RICH, Harvard School of Public Health

The formation of healthy sexuality is one of the challenges of adolescence, and it's one that's been the subject of countless teen dramas from *Romeo and Juliet* all the way up to *Titanic* and *The Fault in Our Stars*. We all remember our own painful milestones from those turbulent years, including awkward first dates and kisses, asking someone to a school dance, the first time we were intimate with someone, etc. all culminating (hopefully) in a healthy, stable lifelong relationship.

What pornography does—if only because the sheer abundance of it today—is give children a *very* skewed view of what a relationship is, how to act in a relationship, what normal sexual behavior constitutes, etc. along with plenty of body image issues and performance issues. The issue is not so much the *material* itself as that sheer *amount* of it, combined with how easily accessible it is to young people during the very same formative years in which they're developing their own sexual identity and sexual interests. Introducing any sort of deviant pornography or deviant sexual behavior to a young person at this age can set them up for deviant—and possibly criminal—interests and behaviors later in life. This is even worse given the fact that, as with drug and alcohol addiction, chronic users of pornography build up a "tolerance" over time, meaning that the amount of pornography required for sexual arousal increases the more a person is exposed to pornography. Over time, this can lead people of all ages to pursue the outer limits of whatever material they come across, from the merely gaudy or offensive to the downright obscene and even criminal.

In our professional work, we've had criminal cases in which a defendant has first been exposed to pornography featuring 12-year-olds when he—and it's usually a he in criminal cases—was 12 years old. At that age, both the viewer and the victim (this is *child* pornography) are peers, so the young viewer is unlikely to think anything of it because with a peer it feels like normal sexual exploration. However, this becomes a problem when that 12-year-old consumer then ages into an 18 or 20-year-old who still views pornography featuring 12 year olds and is now subject to the adult criminal justice system.

"I have also seen in my clinical experience that pornography damages the sexual performance of viewers.
Pornograpy viewers tend to have problems with premature ejaculation and erectile dysfunction. Having spent so much time in unnatural sexual experiences with paper, celluloid, and cyberspace, they seem to find it difficult to have sex with a real human being. Pornography is raising their expectation and demand for types and amounts of sexual experiences;
at the same time it reducing their ability to experience sex."
—DR. MARY ANNE LAYDEN, University of Pennsylvania

154

Pornography

In an ironic twist of fate, this gross overconsumption of pornography not only causes the body image issues we're all familiar with (girls comparing themselves to airbrushed models) but can also cause *performance* issues. The same young people who build up a tolerance from viewing (and pleasuring themselves while watching) pornography, when presented with the opportunity for *actual* sexual intercourse are demonstrating the inability to perform for an actual, flesh and blood partner. Preferring the fake over the real is itself a testament to how pornography today distorts the development of our healthy human sexuality.

Not Exclusively a Boys' Problem

It's a common assumption among parents and among those over a certain age that, as with video games, the consumption of online pornography is an issue only for adolescent and young adult males. But, as with video games, the porn companies are always looking to grow their market share and that of course includes not only international markets and expanded age demographics, but attracting more female viewers as well. According to one large porn website, fully 29% of their viewers in 2018 were female—a three percentage point increase from the previous year—and we can expect that trend to continue with time.

Pornography not only affects those who consume it, but those of us who have to interact with those who consume it as well. In addition to the body image and sexual performance issues, a 2002 study by the American Academy of Matrimonial Lawyers found that 68% of divorces involved one party meeting a new partner over the Internet; 56% involved one party obsessively viewing online pornography; 47% involved excessive computer use; and 33% involved excessive time spent in chat rooms. While it's fair to assume that most of those porn consumers were male, that's not always the case today.

EFFECTS OF PROLONGED EXPOSURE TO PORNOGRAPHY:

- Exaggerated perception of sexual activity in society
- Diminished trust in intimate partners
- Abandonment of hope for monogamy with partners
- Expectation that sexual promiscuity is normal
- Belief that sexual abstinence is unhealthy
- Belief that sexual pleasure can come without affection between partners
- Cynical attitudes towards love
- Belief that marriage is sexually confining
- Less desire to marry and raise a family

Source: *Journal of Adolescent Health*

Females typically begin viewing pornography at a later age than males, although the research specific to females is relatively scarce, and it's dangerous to assume that studies of either males or the population at large are also applicable to females, particularly given the increase in porn viewing with each generation. As we said in the introduction to the book, one of the greatest challenges we face in confronting technology issues is having enough accurate scientific data to not only make informed decisions in our personal lives and clinical practices but also in the broader issue of public policy.

That said, early research specific to teenage girls indicates that girls who consume porn at an earlier age engage in more risky behavior, including alcohol consumption, smoking tobacco, and casual sex. One difference, however, is that the data shows no difference in overall screen time between girls who consume pornography and those who don't, which is a differentiator between porn-consuming boys and those who don't. Porn-consuming girls have also reported problems in relations with peers, which may indicate a weaker social network and social support system than offered to other girls their age.

Strategies for Combating Internet Pornography with Your Children

Start Earlier Than You Think You Need To. As you're now painfully aware, kids' exposure to pornography today begins *long* before the adolescent hormones kick in. Anyone who uses the Internet nowadays is bound to stumble across every sort of offensive material just by virtue of opening a web browser and clicking through pages, while even the best email filtering will still let the occasional unwanted message through. That necessitates "having the conversation" with your kids about the birds and the bees long before you might think you need to, or long before you feel you're ready. *This is one of the largest generational differences you will encounter as a parent.* Remember, kids typically first encounter pornography when they begin writing school reports—the middle of grade school—and porn companies are now trying to introduce their products to young people in inconspicuous ways even at that age—think of the candy cigarettes that stores used to sell and you get the idea.

"From 2003-2010 I edited [men's] magazine *Loaded*. With its frequent nudity and lewd photo spreads, I'd long been accused of being a soft pornographer, and after leaving *Loaded* I agonized that my magazine may have switched a generation onto more explicit online porn… like many parents, I fear that my boy's childhood could be taken away by pornography. So we have to fight back. We need to get tech-savvy, and as toe-curling as it seems, we are the first generation that will have to talk to our children about porn. We have to tell our kids that pornographic sex is fake and real sex is about love, not lust. By talking to them, they stand a chance. If we stick our head in the sand, we are fooling only ourselves."

—MARTIN DAUBNEY, British magazine publisher

Install Filtering Software. The first line of defense against objectionable content is to install good filtering software. As with all things related to technology, filtering software is constantly changing and one program will be better than another based on what kind of devices you use and what your particular needs are. Two good places to begin to look for the best, most current filtering software for your family's devices are CNET.com and Consumer Reports. Be sure to also look for differences between *social media* filtering software and *Internet* filtering software, as they aren't the same, and if your children know they're being screened in one way but not the other, they'll take the path of least resistance.

Since schools today have reached a critical mass in using technology across the curriculum, and many schools also require families to purchase devices for their children, we recommend talking with the tech support staff at your children's school, along with parents of older children, to see what other recommendations they may have. Support staff—because they're always fixing iPad screens for kids who have dropped them or trying to retrieve a lost homework assignment off of a hard drive—will know what games and other trends the kids at your child's school are up to. Additionally, if you work in a traditional office environment, your office's tech support staff will also undoubtedly be a source of good leads on software as well. Lastly, places like the Apple Store and Best Buy's Geek Squad may also be willing to install protections on electronic devices before you let your children use them.

Good filtering software will also have parental controls that will allow you to turn the filters on and off as needed, and also allow or disallow downloads either from individual sites or altogether. Although you'll want to keep filters on 99% of the time, there will be exceptions, such as when your child has to do a school report about breast cancer. Remember the Seinfeld episode about "good naked" and "bad naked:" studying a human cadaver in medical school is not the same thing as watching a peep show in Times Square, and unfortunately filtering software will probably never be 100% effective at discerning the difference.

Watch Their Social Media Accounts. Good filtering software should catch most of the offensive material your children may come across online, but one avenue of pornography that escapes parents' attention is often the most wide-spread use of pornograpy today: social media.

We'll discuss social media more broadly in the next chapter, but as with people in any other industry, adult film stars have material that they want to promote and sell, which is why they're turning to social media to sell products, create buzz, and connect with their customers. In recent years, platforms like Twitter, Instagram, and SnapChat have come under harsh criticism for not providing parents with enough tools to protect their children from exposure to adult material. It's all too common for one child to come across something they believe is naughty, shares it with another friend, who shares it with another friend, until your child sees it. The embedded links on social media pages typically don't use the same sorts of web addresses that adult sites use, and they may not be caught by the filtering software you install on your children's devices. Keep in mind as well that even if your filtering software works 99% of the time, that still means that your child will still be exposed to pornography at some point whether you like it or not.

This is one reason why many parents insist on being added as a "friend" on their child's social media accounts. This way, parents can monitor from time to time what it is that their children are sharing with their friends and keep an eye out for any objectionable material that may come their way. Knowing that mom and dad are keeping an eye on their social media accounts will also remind kids to keep their behavior on the up and up—even if you aren't checking things regularly.

Have Your Children Use Their Devices in Open Spaces. It's harder for your kids to consume pornography or engage in other disreputable online behavior when they know someone might walk by, especially if that someone includes mom and dad. If you have a family computer room, for example, insist that the door remain open so that adults can periodically check in on the kids to see that they are indeed actually doing their homework or playing a game with friends. Yes, your kids will still be able to sneak things behind your back or switch between programs when you're not watching, but the combination of filtering software and checking in will do wonders to reduce the chances of your children seeing this sort of material, as the combination of two methods that are each 99% effective won't completely eliminate the chance of your children seeing inappropriate content, but will further reduce the likelihood.

If you don't have a computer room, then having your kids do their homework either at desks in their room—with the door open, slightly ajar, or at least unlocked—or at the family dinner table will also allow you to check on them to ensure that they're using their devices responsibly. This will be an issue when your kids take their smaller devices everywhere with them, and this again is where good filtering software will help. Also, be sure to give yourself the benefit of the doubt here. Helicopter parents (and worse yet, bulldozer parents) can't be with their children 24/7 and from our work with law enforcement, we can tell you that online predators who talk to kids are typically talking to kids *right out in the open*, and not behind closed doors.

For Children Age 8 and Under. While your children are still innocent and naive, we recommend the simple rule that if they see a naked person on the Internet, computer, or mobile phone, they should let parents or another trusted adult know. If they talk to you about seeing a naked picture or video, have a discussion about what they saw and where they saw the image. If you can discern that your child was exposed to some form of pornography then it's important to inform them that the images and videos they viewed were a form of pretending between adults who are actors. Younger children may have multiple questions about the image or video they viewed and it's okay to talk to them about it, even if you feel extremely uncomfortable. This is where it'll be time for you as a parent to draw on those dormant improvisational skills to pretend that you're not freaked out by having to talk about sex with your kids.

While you don't want to have a sophisticated conversation with them at this age, you do want to make them feel comfortable asking you these important questions. For younger children, you don't have to get into the nitty gritty of sex, but provide a more general version of sex education. There are many excellent books about how to speak to your children about sexual education, so we would encourage you to purchase and read one before you get caught off guard. Another recommendation is to have these conversations as part of normal discussions, rather than as "special discussions." If you discuss these topics as they occur organically, then your children might be more comfortable bringing questions to you in the future.

THE 3 AWKWARD, MUST-HAVE CONVERSATIONS

Sexual Development: boys and girls are different
Sex Education: sex is a healthy part of adult relationships
Pornography: it's everywhere but it's not real

For Children Age 11 and Over. Building on earlier conversations with your kids, remind them that pornography is NOT real intercourse between two loving, consenting adults. For the actors, it's nothing more than a job, and for the companies involved, it's a lucrative business run by multimillionaires who are completely indifferent to the effects it may be having on your child.. Ask your children if they have any concerns about what they have seen. It is also important to ask what they are looking at and whether they have viewed any child pornography. This should all be discussed in the context that kids are naturally curious about sex, and just because they have seen pornography does not mean that they will become a sex addict. In fact, the same curiosity that drove boys to seek out Playboys decades ago is the same curiosity that drives kids today to seek out pornography online. Just know that viewing pornography is normal and that kids are naturally curious about sex.

Explain to Your Children the Human Cost of Pornography. As a general rule, people don't have sex on camera for money for good reasons. While a certain percentage of adult film actors are well-adjusted exhibitionists, unfortunately, the ugly reality is that that industry is a haven for lost souls. As with traditional Hollywood, behind the facade of beautiful people—voluptuous women and well endowed men—lies a tremendous amount of sadness. In the case of porn, that includes more than a few people from broken families who were molested as children, never finished school, are desperate financially, have spent time in prison, and have all sorts of unresolved emotional issues, which together culminate in their having sex with strangers in front of a digital video camera for a few hundred dollars. That video then makes its way around the world on the Internet and haunts them for the rest of their lives, as it's a genie that can never be put back in the bottle. News reports in Southern California and South Florida regularly feature stories of former adult performers who went on to build normal lives for themselves, only to be fired from jobs and publicly shamed for having been part of the adult industry in previous years. Ironically, many adult stars have retired to Utah, where the Mormon Church has pushed for some of the strongest anti-pornography laws in the country, which allows former adult stars to live in relative peace and anonymity.

The pay for adult performers today isn't what people think it is, performers are often released by the industry after only a few months, sexually transmitted diseases are rampant, performers typically moonlight as prostitutes, and many turn to drug use even when not working, to numb themselves to the reality of their day to day lives. Although the people involved may be physically attractive, the work they're involved in can be anything but. And even when your children aren't handing over your credit card information to view pornography online, the mere act of clicking through those sites generates advertising dollars that support the porn industry and the exploitation behind it.

Pornography

- Porn is a $97 billion industry today, responsible for 35% of Internet downloads.

- The porn industry is consistently at the forefront of technology innovation.

- Ease of access and the sheer volume of material available distinguishes today's porn.

- Children are typically first exposed to online porn by age 8 and many develop a daily viewing habit by age 11.

- Females constitute 29% of porn viewers and the number is growing.

- Chronic porn viewing causes sexual performance issues.

ACTION STEPS

- Be prepared to talk with your kids about the birds and the bees earlier than your parents did with you.

- Consider installing filtering software on your children's devices.

- Have your children use their devices in public places.

- Communicate your values and expectations with your children.

FOR FURTHER READING

- *Beyond Birds and Bees: Bringing Home a New Message to Our Kids About Sex, Love, and Equality*, by Bonnie J. Rough

- *It's Perfectly Normal: Changing Bodies, Growing Up, Sex, and Sexual Health*, by Robie H. Harris

- *The Pornography Industry: What Everyone Needs to Know*, by Dr. Shira Tarrant

CHAPTER TWELVE

Social Media and Cyberbullying

"To this day, the boy that used to bully me at school still takes my lunch money. On the plus side, he makes great Subway sandwiches."

—DIPLY

O NE OF THE MOST PAINFUL AND SHOCKING STATISTICS TO come out of our work with kids in issues of technology overuse is that according to some studies, the suicide rate for girls aged 10-14 has risen 200% in the past decade. For boys, it has "only" risen by 50%. This phenomenon even has a name now—"bullycide," for suicide due to bullying. More specifically, due to cyberbullying.

Behind those statistics are real people. As adults, we all know that kids are cruel, and we all carry scars from our own childhoods of things that were said to us on the playground, comments about us that we overheard other people making, or not being invited to the right party. But today are playing on a whole other level:

- 43% of kids have been bullied online; 1 in 4 have had it happen more than once

- 70% of students report seeing frequent bullying online
- 68% of teens agree that cyberbullying is a serious problem
- Only 1 in 10 children will inform a parent or trusted adult of of their abuse
- Girls are twice as likely as boys to engage in or be victims of cyberbullying
- 75% of students admit to having visited a website bashing another student
- Bullying victims are 2-9 times more likely to consider suicide

Source: DoSomething.org

What Exactly is Cyberbullying?

Cyberbullying takes on many forms, and on a basic level can be defined as bullying or harassment using electronic means. One of the biggest challenges we face is simply *defining* what we're dealing with, which then allows us to find good data, scale up best practices, and generate informed, effective public policy. Some of today's most common forms of cyberbullying include:

- **Exclusion:** Deliberately leaving someone out of plans, conversations, etc. coordinated online
- **Harassment:** A general catchall for repeatedly inflicting emotional pain on someone online
- **Outing/Doxing:** Revealing sensitive information online about another person without consent for the purpose of embarrassing or humiliating them
- **Trickery:** Befriending a target to gain trust and then revealing trusted information to third parties
- **Cyberstalking:** One or more bullies gathering information about a person, frightening or threatening him or her across multiple platforms, and potentially crossing into physical stalking
- **Fraping:** Taking over someone else's social media profile and posting inappropriate content without consent

- **Masquerading:** Creating fake email accounts or social media profiles in the name of another person to create false impressions and corrupt relationships
- **Dissing:** Spreading cruel information about another person to ruin that person's reputation or relationships with other people.
- **Trolling:** Posting inflammatory comments to upset someone, by a perpetrator somewhat detached from the victim.
- **Flaming:** Directly sending insults/profanity or posting about the victim to incite online fights.

Sources: Securly software company, Cyberbullying Research Center

Cyberbullying is perhaps the worst scourge of today's children's lives. Children have always been cruel, but the anonymity of the online world makes it that much easier for immature children to inflict *devastating* damage on each other with long term consequences, the likes of which they don't fully comprehend. Even we *adults* sometimes forget that there's another person on the other end of our online interactions; our *children* are going to grasp this even less than we do. In the meantime, our kids will make their youthful mistakes while we adults, the digital immigrants, will never fully understand our children's online inner lives, particularly in this realm.

Why is Cyberbullying Uniquely Bad?

All bullying is painful, and many of us carry deep, visceral scars from our own childhood experiences. But several factors make this new generation of cyberbullying particularly bad. Particular issues include:

- Cyberbullying happens away from adults. Your kid can be on their iPad right in the living room having their heart torn to shreds and you won't know about it. At school, an athletic practice, recess, or study hall, adult supervisors are there to monitor the interaction among kids, but online very few moderators exist anywhere, and often the damage has already been done by the time any offensive content is recognized or removed.

167

- Cyberbullying can be done anonymously. One person can destroy another person's life and reputation without the victim ever knowing who the perpetrator is, making any remediation difficult to impossible.
- Cyberbullying can easily reach a mass audience. All it takes is a few strokes on the keyboard and the click of a mouse to reach thousands of people.
- Cyberbullying can be done anywhere. Geography and proximity no longer matter.

Source: Pacer Center / National Bullying Prevention Center

We would add Permanency to that list—the internet is forever, while the slings and arrows we suffered as children, though they may live on in our memories, have no lasting, tangible existence.

Targets for Cyberbullying

As with real life bullying, cyberbullying victims are kids who, for one reason or another don't fit in. This includes, but is not limited to, the kids who might wear glasses, have excessive acne, are socially awkward, aren't popular, or who are depressed and have low self-esteem. There are three groups of kids, however, who are disproportionately subject to much more cyberbullying.

LGBTQ and Other Non-Binary Children

As we discussed in the previous chapter, one big part of adolescent development is the discovery and exploration of our sexuality, and if that weren't already corrupted enough by today's profusion of pornography, it's that much more difficult for kids who don't conform to traditional gender binaries and the stereotypical gender roles that go along with them. It does "get better," but first kids have to get through those painful years.

Data today are showing that sexual minority youth are twice as likely to be cyberbullied and that this bullying typically comes from members of the same sex. The good news for LGBTQ kids is that the online world can provide them with resources to build a supportive peer group to help deal with the day to day struggles they may be facing, particularly in the parts of the country that may not generally be accepting of their differences.

RESOURCES FOR LGBTQ KIDS AND PARENTS:

The Trevor Project: Provides crisis intervention and suicide prevention for LGBTQ youth under the age of 25

It Gets Better Project: Provides resources for LGBT youth and teens

Gay-Straight Alliance Clubs: Offered in many schools today

Gay, Lesbian, and Straight Education Network: Provides resources to create inclusive K-12 schools

PFLAG—Parents and Friends of Lesbians and Gays: Support network of family, friends, and allies of LGBTQ children and adults

Autism Spectrum Disorders

The increase of Autism Spectrum Disorders is one of the public health challenges of our time, now affecting an estimated 1 in 59 children (four times more likely in boys than girls). In terms of bullying and cyberbullying, one of the most difficult issues that parents face is that their ASD children won't necessarily understand the social cues that tell them that they are being bullied (even as we parents are likely to explode with rage at the sight of our children being humiliated), nor are they necessarily aware of the need to reach out to others when that bullying does occur. It simply may not occur to ASD kids that other people might be experiencing things differently or that the way they're being treated isn't fair.

Important in working with kids on the spectrum who're being cyberbullied is to approach the topic delicately and on their terms, giving them space as they may be feeling heightened emotions and not understand that bullying is not their fault. This can be all the more difficult given the preference that some ASD kids have for communication using electronic devices (much easier for them than face to face interaction) and the reticence they may have towards the calming touch and hug that we all would otherwise want to give someone who's hurting. The data on cyberbullying and children on the Autism Spectrum are still very fresh, and best practices are still being researched, so consultation with a professional who works with ASD children might be necessary.

RESOURCES FOR AUTISM SPECTRUM KIDS AND PARENTS

Autism Speaks: National autism foundation offers a wealth of resources

Digitability: Teaches technology skills and literacy to ASD kids and schools

Weight Issues

One last common victim of cyberbullying, and a longtime victim in American schools, is the overweight child. One of the more recent examples of this thus far was one that didn't happen in school but no doubt dredged up the feelings of every overweight child grown into adulthood, when Playboy magazine's 2015 Playmate of the Year, Dani Mathers, sent out a picture on Snapchat of an anonymous overweight 70-year-old woman changing clothes in an L.A. Fitness locker room. In one half of the photo was Mathers with her hand covering her mouth in disbelief, while the other half showed the woman with the caption, "If I can't unsee this then you can't either."

The Dani Mathers case was but one prominent example of this—in a well-publicized case, she was ultimately sentenced to 30 days of community service and 3 years of probation for her actions—but fat shaming has been an issue on the Internet for years. Many forums and websites have been maliciously created and have *thousands* of followers mocking pictures of overweight individuals followed by insulting, hurtful comments directed at the overweight individuals pictured.

Although bullying can often be broken down across all sorts of demographic groups (i.e. poorer kids in a wealthy school), overweight kids are likely to be bullied in school no matter what their demographic background. In middle school, 30% of overweight girls experience bullying on a daily basis as do 24% of boys, and by high school those numbers double to 63% of girls and 58% of boys. Not surprising, for overweight kids, this can then lead to eating disorders, along with the usual depression, anxiety, and other mental illnesses.

RESOURCES FOR OVERWEIGHT KIDS AND PARENTS

Obesity Action Coalition: provides educational resources to counter weight shaming

World Obesity Foundation: dedicated to education and policy development to reduce obesity

UConn Rudd Center for Food Policy and Obesity: dedicated to fostering healthy living, a healthy food supply, and combating weight shaming

How Cyberbullying Affects Bullies, Victims, and Communities

The adolescent brain doesn't handle shocks or stresses nearly as well as the adult brain does. As adults, we're able to shake off the sorts of stressors that can sometimes rock a child to the core of his or her being, as in the story of Gavin, who shared with friends a meme that he didn't realize was racist. Past a certain age, adults understand that we all make mistakes, that we don't all get along with each other, different strokes for different folks, live and let live, etc., but our children haven't yet learned life's lessons, which in part is why bullying is such a painful, hurtful experience—made all the worse by technology.

SIGNS YOUR CHILD IS BEING CYBERBULLIED

- Being upset after using the Internet or cell phone
- Unwilling to talk about online activities or phone use
- Friends disappearing, or being excluded from social events
- Spending much more or much less time texting, gaming, or using social media
- Many new phone numbers, texts, or email addresses show up on his or her devices
- Seeming withdrawn, upset, or outraged after texting or being online
- Not wanting to go to school, or avoiding friends and classmates
- Avoiding formerly enjoyable social situations
- Fresh marks on the skin, indicative of self-harm
- Changes in personality—anger, depression, crying, etc.
- Difficulty sleeping
- Low self-esteem

Sources: United Kingdom Department of Education, Family Lives

For the child being bullied, the effects are devastating—and may be a reason why many of you bought this book in the first place. But what's been studied much less is the effect that both bullying and cyberbullying has on the child *engaged* in the act of bullying. For those children, it can become a vicious cycle akin to domestic violence or alcoholism, handed down from one generation to the next, and which they only fully appreciate long after the fact—after the damage has been done to themselves and to others. In the meantime, hurting, broken children (more likely to get into fights, to steal property, to drink alcohol and smoke cigarettes, and get bad grades in school) continue to pass along their hurt and pain to other children like a disease infecting society and, as Gandhi said, "An eye for an eye leaves the whole world blind." This is why it's so important to intervene in cases of bullying—to prevent other children from being hurt, and to find ways to heal the pain that causes a child to lash out in the first place before it becomes a mass contagion in a community.

It may not be easy to operate from a position of empathy for the child engaged in bullying, considering how devastating it can be for the child who's the target of such viciousness. First and foremost, because the attacks happen online—and children today are almost always connected to technology—this means that your kids literally *do not have any safe space away from online bullying* unless they completely step away from technology—and we all know how difficult and unlikely that is. When bullying was limited to person to person contact, kids could count on time at home or with friends as safe time away from aggressors. Sadly, this option no longer exists.

Thus far, cyberbullying has been shown to dramatically affect children's self-esteem, cause heightened anxiety, and potentially lead to addictive and obsessive behaviors. In the cases in which it's anonymous, children can feel overwhelmed, vulnerable, and powerless. Declines in school performance, skipping school, dropping out of school, self-isolation, etc. are not at all uncommon. Kids may also feel physical symptoms like stress headaches, ulcers, and skin rashes due to the stress they're feeling. Depending on the child, this can also result in your child's internalizing those feelings in the form of sadness or result in his or her lashing out at other students, and in turn becoming a bully and continuing the cycle.

Lastly, kids who *witness* cyberbullying may not understand that they have a role to play here, too. The mere act of witnessing cyberbullying can leave other children feeling fearful and powerless to act, or to feel guilty for not acting or to be tempted to participate in the bullying. They need to understand that *silence is consent*, and that *everyone* has a role to play in eliminating bullying, both online and off.

TOP 10 TIPS FOR TEENS TO STAND UP TO CYBERBULLIES

- **Report Incidents to Your School.** Many schools are now implementing anonymous reporting systems to address bullying in all its forms. Particularly if the bullying involves anything related to your child's school, such as taking place over school wifi, then the school has a right to be involved and it can be dealt with within the school system.

- **Collect Evidence.** Take screenshots, save images or messages, or screen record whatever you observe. If disciplinary measures requiring school or law enforcement are required, then concrete evidence will be needed by authorities to document what exactly has happened.

- **Report Incidents to Site/App Developers.** Developers are on your side and all have a vested interest in creating safe and welcoming environments for their users. Users who violate their terms of use can be removed immediately.

- **Talk to a Trusted Adult.** Relationships with teachers, counselors, coaches, family friends, or even older siblings can help children vent whenever something negative happens online, especially when kids think their parents won't understand.

- **Demonstrate Care.** Reach out to friends of yours who are being bullied. Make positive comments on their pages, send them kind text messages, and let them know at school that you have their back.

- **Work Together.** Gather your friends together in support of any friend being cyberbullied. Let your friend know that they are loved and supported. Use strength in numbers so your friend doesn't feel isolated.

- **Tell Them to Stop.** If you know the person engaged in cyberbullying, tell them to stop. Have your other friends tell them to stop. Remember that *silence is consent*, so if your child doesn't say anything, they are inadvertently telling bullies that their behavior is acceptable.

- **Don't Encourage It.** Don't make comments on bullying pages, don't add emojis in comments, don't gossip, and don't stand on the sidelines.

- **Stay Safe.** Don't put yourself in harm's way. When emotions are running high, walk away. Resist escalating situations. Stay away from places where people are cruel to each other. And *never* physically threaten others.

- **Don't Give Up.** This is a battle that's just begun. Work with friends, classmates, teachers, and parents to brainstorm new tactics to create a welcoming environment in your school and community.

Source: Cyberbullying Research Center

Strategies for Combating Cyberbullying

"School administrators can't say it's up to the parents. Parents can't say it's up to the teachers. Teachers can't say it's not their job. And kids can't say, 'I was too afraid to tell.' Every single one of us has to play our role if we're serious about putting an end to the madness. We are all responsible. We must be."

—MEGAN KELLEY HALL

Teach Your Children That Everything Said Online is Permanent

This may be one of the most important lessons we can pass along in this book.

Although efforts have been undertaken in Europe (through laws and litigation over a new "right to be forgotten") to change this, any time anyone shares anything on the Internet, it goes out into cyberspace for eternity. This is not even because tech companies are compiling data on consumers or because companies refuse to delete data from their servers, or even because "temporary" forms of social media lie about deleting pictures after a certain period of time but because of how the Internet was first designed in the 1960s.

The Internet is a decentralized network of computers—a network of networks—which passes data from one computer to another like a hot potato. Unfortunately, that means that bits of data are sent across computers all across the world without your knowing. Consequently, even if a picture is posted to social media—and then deleted—*it's still out there somewhere*, and that means that someone somewhere, if they're so motivated, can find whatever it is that you post online.

Virtual private networks ("VPNs") are emerging as a possible solution to this problem—you interact with the Internet through a company that you pay to anonymize your data. This is a great option for parent devices (as you pay your bills online and put personal information out in cyberspace) and can help protect children's devices and data as well. However, the downside is losing the ability to use monitoring software on their Internet searches. This is a painful trade-off that needs to be considered as although you may be able to protect your child's identity online, you run the risk of letting them view pornography. And if that sounds frustrating, we agree with you.

Don't Be in a Rush to Get Your Child a Smartphone

We optimistically hope that "dumb" phones make their way back into the mainstream culture. In Hollywood, having a basic flip phone or something similarly vanilla is already a status symbol, for people famous and successful enough to *not* need to be connected to the Internet or to check emails at all hours of the day—that's what they have assistants for. Meanwhile, as all of us regular folk have experienced, in an effort to cram as many functions into a phone as possible, cell phone manufacturers often neglect that whole "phone" part of a smartphone. Being able to play Candy Crush or Fortnite may be great, but not if the device you're carrying all day long drops calls when you're on the road, or if you find yourself in the middle of Midtown Manhattan and can't get a signal. That defeats the whole purpose of carrying a "phone" in the first place.

As your children grow older, they'll want a phone to get in touch with their friends, and you'll probably want them to have a phone so you can stay in contact and coordinate activities, especially if you have multiple children who are each involved in multiple activities in multiple locations, and it falls on you to coordinate a mish mash of different schedules. *You have options in choosing phones,* and it doesn't have to have the latest bells and whistles. Smartphones all have excellent functionality but cross the line from "tool" to "toy" rather quickly. Particularly for younger children, a good, basic, vanilla phone will do the trick, with calling, texting, and basic web services. You'll undoubtedly save plenty of money on the data plan, as well.

For the most current reviews of cell phones and blocking apps, we recommend visiting CNET.com and Consumer Reports.

Use Blocking Apps to Limit Your Children's Social Media Time

Blocking apps are another newer tool to help you oversee your children's use of social media. These are now being built into both devices and offered by service providers to allow you to restrict the amount of time and which particular social media sites your children use. The younger your child, the more we recommend using these tools. Keep in mind that your children won't really "need" a social media account until they start looking for adult jobs in their late teens and need to set up a LinkedIn account. That isn't the case for a 12 year old!

"Facebook has revealed their estimated net worth—$96 billion. That's almost as much money as businesses lose every year from their employees wasting time looking at Facebook."
—JAY LENO

Switch Your Phones Over to Black and White Displays

It's not an accident that this is difficult to do on most smartphones… because it's one of the most effective ways to minimize frivolous use of phones and other devices.

While we all like to believe that we humans are highly evolved, sophisticated creatures, we're still attracted to pretty colors and flashy lights just like our biological cousins located a few rungs below us on the evolutionary ladder. It's not an accident that we mentioned Las Vegas and Atlantic City slot machines early in the book—because your phones really do stimulate the brain like a miniature version of the Las Vegas Strip, right in your pocket every day.

Switching your phone to a black and white (or "grayscale") display will allow you to keep the same functionality in your phone and other devices, but it takes away the pretty colors. This means that we're much more likely to use our devices for *information* rather than *entertainment*. You and your children can still check emails, send text messages, make phone calls, surf the web, etc. but the pretty, distracting colors will be taken away.

While this varies by device, we recommend a quick Google search or checking in at your local cellular provider store for advice on how to do this on your family's devices.

Don't Install Social Media Apps on Devices

This may seem counterintuitive at first—we're not saying that your kids can't use social media—but that social media *apps* are some of the most guilty offenders in harvesting data from unsuspecting users. You and your children can still use social media on your phones, but by logging in *through your phone's web browser* you will be able not only to avoid installing large, clunky, memory-hogging software, but also one link in the multiverse of tracking services that place targeted ads on every platform of every device you use.

One personal favorite of ours is the "Lite" version of Facebook. Originally designed for third world countries with limited cellular data bandwidth, the Lite version of Facebook still allows users to connect to the site, scroll through their news feed, message with friends and other contacts, etc. but without installing either the large Facebook app or its companion Messenger app, the latter of which has been documented to listen in on users' conversations at random points in the day.

Let Your Children Blame You for Not Participating in Online Activities

As we all know, our younger children will generally do whatever tasks that we and other adults ask of them. With our teenagers, that's a different story. The backtalk and attitude that they give us is an unfortunate part of their growing up and differentiating themselves from their parents, to find out who they are as people.

Your kids will always be subject to peer pressure in one form or another—we adults are also subject to peer pressure—and one of the best ways for your children to defuse that pressure is for you to allow them to blame you whenever they're not allowed to do something that you don't want them to be doing.

If there's a big party that all the cool kids are going to and you don't want your kids going, let your kids tell everyone that you need them to babysit, or perform chores around the house, or that they're grounded. If there's a particular app that you don't want your children using, or a game you won't let them play, then *let your children blame you*. Better to have your children angry at you (briefly) than to have them subject to whatever outside forces you don't want interfering in their development. Letting them blame you also shifts the burden onto you as the parent (we trust this is the least of your worries), while your child will suffer less of the social alienation that could otherwise come from not participating in a certain game, activity, or app.

Teach Your Kids to Never Share Their Passwords

One of the worst, most underhanded forms of cyberbullying today is the hijacking of another person's social media accounts. When children are careless with their passwords—and haven't set up the necessary password retrieval methods and security blocks—that opens the door for other kids to impersonate your children online. As with actual identity theft, this can be incredibly damaging and hurtful to both your children and your family's reputation for years to come. Since much of social media operates as a "closed" system in which everyone is keeping up appearances, with your children and their friends intimately connected to each other, whenever those accounts are compromised and offensive posts are made in your children's names, the effects can be instantaneous, devastating, and long-lasting. We *strongly* recommend teaching your children to *only* share their passwords with you—their parents—and to *not* keep password lists with them, particularly when they leave the house. Having any sort of master password list for a child is simply asking for trouble, should it ever be misplaced or fall into the wrong hands, unless it is maintained securely at home.

Don't Engage with Bullies Online

Easier said than done, teach your kids to not "friend" or "follow" kids that they know are bullying other kids. The less of an audience there is for an online bully, the less likely they are to engage in that behavior. Every time your child interacts online with someone engaging in disreputable behavior, your child is tacitly endorsing that person and his or her behavior. Giving likes, shares, retweets, etc. to that person crosses the line from bystander to supporter, which can make the situation even worse for the children being bullied. If your child has already "friended" a bully online, he or she doesn't necessarily have to unfriend that person, either. Your child can simply un-follow or hide that person, to avoid the possible confrontation that could come from deleting someone online.

Take Screenshots

In cases of bullying, use the screenshot features built into your children's devices to capture whatever bullying statements are made to them by other children. Although your kids will want to delete things right away to hide the damage, having evidence of actual bullying incidents will help you as a parent should matters rise to the level of involving either school or law enforcement officials. Having a few extra megabytes of data uploaded to the cloud will save you and your child from having to engage in "he said / she said" arguments with school administrators, law enforcement, and other parents—should matters ever come to that.

Be a Friend to Kids Being Bullied

If your child witnesses another child being bullied, in addition to the previously mentioned strategies, it's important to reach out and *be a friend* to kids who are being bullied. The simple act of grace of letting a kid in pain know that they're loved and thought of by other children is something that the other child (and their parents) will never forget. Equally important is to let the bully know that his or her behavior is unacceptable, whether by having your child speak to the child doing the bullying, or to involve school officials if necessary. We realize that this is a very difficult step for any child due to their fear of becoming the next target. However, standing up to bullies is an important skill for all of us to develop, and the younger the better.

If Your Child is the Bully

Unfortunately, this can be a wakeup call for parents, because the previous content about other kids bullying your child (acting out over issues at home) can also be true of your own child. If your kids are acting out and mistreating other children, this can be a prime teachable moment for them about good behavior, and not only the "Golden Rule" (treat others like *you* would want to be treated) but also the "Platinum Rule" (treat others like *they* would want to be treated). You may also want to reevaluate whether you've been able to spend enough quality time with your child so that he or she is developing appropriately both socially and emotionally in addition to physically and academically. As parents, we're constantly torn in different directions between work, family, and community responsibilities, and that means that whether we agree with it or not, our kids are bound to feel neglected from time to time. Finally, children who bully others online have demonstrated that they do not have the requisite maturity to handle an electronic device or social media account, and these should be removed. An important principle to remember is that *there are separate realities in every family*, meaning that your kids will experience things differently than you do, regardless of the underlying reality. That's why you need to be the parent and find out what's wrong.

Some Additional Thoughts on YouTube

As Internet bandwidth has continued to expand this century, the sophistication of material available to kids has grown exponentially. In particular, this has made YouTube grow from a small curiosity to one of the most popular and frequently visited sites on the Internet, with a universe worth of material and comments sections that consistently bring out the best and worst in people.

With your children, we recommend no YouTube or no unsupervised You-Tube for your younger children, and to turn on YouTube's restricted mode for the devices your older children will use unsupervised. If you come across any offensive content on the site, be sure to report it to site administrators and tell other parents about it, since offensive material will no doubt go viral among your children's friends and classmates.

Social Media and Cyberbullying

KEY TAKEAWAYS FROM THIS CHAPTER

- 3 billion people use social media every month, including 73% of American teens.
- Social media users are often more lonely and isolated than the general population.
- *Everyone* puts up a front on social media.
- 43% of kids have been bullied online; only 1 in 10 will inform a parent or other adult.
- Bullying victims are 2-9 times more likely to consider suicide.
- Bullying is typically caused by problems in the bully's life and has little to do with the victim.

ACTION STEPS

- Teach your children that everything said online is permanent.
- Don't be in a rush to get your child a smartphone.
- Use blocking apps to limit social media use.
- Switch your phones and other devices to black and white displays.
- Let your children blame you for not participating in online activities.
- Teach your kids to never share their passwords.
- Take screenshots of any cyberbullying incidents.

FOR FURTHER READING

- *The Bully, The Bullied, and the Not-So-Innocent Bystander* by Barbara Coloroso
- *Bullies, Cyberbullies and Frenemies* by Michelle Elliott
- *This is a Book for Parents of Gay Kids* by Dannielle Owens-Reid and Kristin Russo
- *Asperger Syndrome and Bullying: Strategies and Solutions* by Nick Dubin
- *Unwritten Rules of Social Relationships: Decoding Social Mysteries Through the Unique*
- *Perspectives of Autism* by Temple Grandin and Sean Barron

CHAPTER THIRTEEN

Children with Unique Needs

"Everyone is a genius, but if you judge a fish by its ability to climb a tree, it will live its whole life thinking it's stupid."

—ALBERT EINSTEIN

There's No Such Thing as a Normal Child

From the time we first find out that we're going to be parents, we know that our lives will never be the same. Although we don't have a say in the children that we're given, we sure as heck are going to have a say in how well they'll be able to navigate the world, particularly after we're gone.

Every child presents a unique set of challenges, because there's no set formula for guiding a human being from a newborn infant into a functioning, well-adjusted, happy, contented, and prosperous young adult. There are simply so many variables at play—each child has different innate abilities, interests, and challenges, and they have to be navigated within our own unique set of circumstances, e.g. available time, financial resources, etc. Parenting is one of the most challenging yet rewarding experiences that we will ever have. That doesn't make it easy, and all of the dramatic scientific advances we've drawn upon in this book still can't account for the judgment calls we all have to make on a daily basis. But they can help!

Here, we want to address a number of particular challenges faced by a large number of parents today, similar to the cases of LGBTQ kids, Autism Spectrum kids, and overweight kids that we highlighted in the chapter on cyberbullying. Think of them as "perfect storms" of technology usage issues coupled with medical and/or developmental challenges. The challenges we outline here are simply a compendium of some of the most common challenges facing parents today, and how we can all integrate some best practices into helping our kids manage their technology as best they can.

Not surprisingly, this was the most difficult chapter for us to write in the book, because there are still so many gaps in the research. As you might expect, there's plenty of medical research on how cigarette smoking affects middle class white men in the suburbs of America, but there isn't nearly as much high quality data on how handheld electronic devices affect the developing brains of children on the Autism Spectrum or with a particular learning disability, let alone around the world and between different demographic groups.

Neurodevelopmental Disorders

"You can do what I cannot do. I can do what you cannot do. Together we can do great things."
—MOTHER THERESA

An important thing to remember about each of these "conditions" is that in another context, it could also be described as a "trait" as well—a child on the Autism Spectrum may struggle to interact with other children, yet have superior raw cognitive firepower. A child with ADHD may be unable to focus for extended periods of time and yet be able to focus brilliantly for short bursts of time. A trait that may be considered a weakness in one arena can be considered a tremendous advantage in another. For example, the legendary swimmer Michael Phelps was ruthlessly teased on the playground as a child for his long arms, and yet in the swimming pool that same physique allowed him to become one of the best Olympians in history.

The many variables that go into raising a child can include any of the varied mental health issues that he or she may face along the way. The DSM-5 is a thick book, just like the *Physician's Desk Reference*, *Gray's Anatomy* (the book, not the TV show), or *Black's Law Dictionary*, and one of the biggest issues for us in offering clinical advice is simply being able to define what we're working with—both the technology itself and also the specific way it interacts with each child's particular neurology. The neurodevelopmental section of today's DSM-5 encompasses a broad range of conditions including Intellectual Disabilities, Communication Disorders, Autism Spectrum Disorders, Attention Deficit/Hyperactivity Disorders, Specific Learning Disorders, Motor Disorders, and Other Neurodevelopmental Disorders. Breaking down each of these would be beyond the scope of this book so we recommend consulting with a mental health professional for a more comprehensive breakdown or any issue specific to your situation. That said, we will take a brief look at some of the more common conditions and how technology overuse can impact them.

Autism Spectrum Disorders

"Stop thinking about normal...You don't have a big enough imagination for what your child can become."
—JOHNNY SEITZ, autistic tightrope artist

Autism Spectrum Disorders are some of the most prevalent issues facing parents today. Autism Spectrum diagnoses have exploded in recent decades, although the root causes are still the subject of research and debate. Thus far, research seems to indicate that genetics and abnormal brain development contribute to the development of this condition.

How Technology Affects Children on the Autism Spectrum

For kids on the Autism Spectrum in particular, technology is truly a mixed blessing. Although they may struggle to interact socially in the real world, ASD kids can enjoy a rich and fulfilling life within the world of technology, which serves as a safe space for them away from the challenges that they face integrating with people in person. The problem for parents is that because ASD kids struggle socially, they tend to retreat to their devices and can fall even further behind in their social development. If left unchecked, this can quickly become a vicious cycle of social struggle and isolation.

Research today is showing that ASD kids have a greater risk for developing addictions simply because their brains have weaker connections between neurons. The same technology that's designed to addict or entice someone with traditional "neurotypical" brain wiring can exacerbate the core problems ASD kids face in innovating, improvising, reflecting, anticipating, evaluating logic, processing things in context, and developing insight and empathy. ASD kids are innately prone to anxiety and compulsive behavior, and today's generation of technology only makes things worse. Both ASD adults and children are at risk for excessive video game usage and developing addictions to pornography, given their increased inability to put down their devices. Excessive screen time can even result in ASD kids regressing developmentally due to a lack of engagement with the real world, and even lead to violence or self-harm—particularly when their parents try to take away their devices.

Finally, remember that kids on the Autism Spectrum are disproportionate victims of cyberbullying today. This makes your job as a parent that much more difficult, because ASD kids innately derive so much pleasure from using electronic devices, yet they may not necessarily comprehend the bullying is being directed their way. Given how the online world is typically such an inviting, safe space for them, they may doubly resent your imposition into their comfort zone. If that sounds like a contradictory observation—that ASD kids find particular pleasure interacting in the digital world, but they are at greater risk of addiction and cyberbullying—that's because it is. It's a particularly difficult Goldilocks Zone for parents of ASD kids to find.

How We Can Manage Technology for Kids on the Autism Spectrum

First and foremost, there are great online resources for ASD kids that can undoubtedly help. Parents with kids on the Autism Spectrum should focus on steering their kids towards technology that has a safe *prosocial* element to it. Given how much ASD kids enjoy technology—and have trouble interacting with people—their use of technology gives parents a perfect opportunity to use technology to help them learn social skills and build friendship networks.

Remember, we do not hate Silicon Valley, and this is one area in which the tech industry is actually stepping up to the plate and helping to provide a new generation of tools, as with the education system in general, to help ASD kids integrate into the world. As parents, it's our challenge to simply steer our kids towards the *right* technology, and consulting with ASD professionals is a great way to start finding the best tools specific to our kids' particular developmental needs.

Be Consistent. ASD kids in particular can get upset very quickly at changes to their routines. No matter what you decide to do in parenting your ASD child's technology use, be consistent. Disruptions in routine can cause outbursts and emotional pain in ASD kids.

TEN THINGS EVERY CHILD WITH AUTISM WISHES YOU KNEW

- I am first and foremost a child. I have autism. I am not primarily "autistic."
- My sensory perceptions are disordered.
- Please remember to distinguish between won't (I choose not to) and can't (I am not able to).
- I am a concrete thinker. This means I interpret language very literally.
- Please be patient with my limited vocabulary.
- Because language is so difficult for me, I am very visually oriented.
- Please focus and build on what I can do rather than what I can't do.
- Please help me with social interactions.
- Try to identify what triggers my meltdowns.
- If you are a family member, please love me unconditionally.

Source: Ellen Notbohm, writer and novelist

Buy Monitoring Software. Remember to be the parent here and invest in software that will allow you to keep tabs on what your child is doing online and with their other technology. Lots of software and apps can run in the background on your children's devices and send you usage reports to keep you informed as to what your children are and aren't doing on their devices. This will allow you to be both proactive and reactive to your children's experiences with technology—trust, but verify. We recommend checking with CNET.com as well as the national ASD organizations for the most current recommendations for the technology you and your family are using.

Look for Engaging, Social, Educational Games. While the engaging and educational parts are good for any child, finding the right games for your ASD kids—ones that have a *social* component—help them to develop that side of their personality in a way that they may not otherwise do. Using technology to help your ASD kids develop socially provides a great way for them to learn in a way that makes them forget that they're learning.

Beware of Cyberbullying. Kids on the Autism Spectrum are much more likely to be targets of cyberbullying, along with LGBTQ kids and overweight kids. The difference is that LGBTQ kids and overweight kids aren't as likely to be married to their devices, which makes it much more important for you to police your ASD children's online presence, behavior, and social networks. We strongly recommend that you educate yourself about the particulars of whatever technology your child uses and the online networks he or she belongs to, and then talk to other parents of ASD kids to find out what your children are all experiencing online. This in particular is a tightrope that you'll have to walk in raising your kids, and there's no easy solution.

RESOURCES FOR PARENTS WITH AUTISM SPECTRUM CHILDREN

Autism Speaks: national advocacy and support group

Asperger and Autism Network (AANE): provides support services

Asperger Syndrome and High Functioning Autism Association: provides phone consultations and support meetings

Southwest Autism Research and Resource Center (SARRC): non-profit provides lifelong support for ASD families and partners in research nationally

Dr. Temple Grandin: renowned professor/author at Colorado State University with autism

Autism Parenting Magazine: British magazine available in print and online

---

Attention Deficit Disorders

Besides Autism Spectrum Disorders, one of the most common developmental issues facing parents and children today is Attention Deficit. Attention Deficit Disorder and Attention Deficit/Hyperactivity Disorder (ADD and AD/HD) together affect 4-6% of the U.S. population, with males three times more likely to be diagnosed than females. Symptoms include inattention, distractibility, fear, anxiety, slow cognitive thinking, daydreaming, procrastination, and poor memory retrieval. The hyperactive component is also much more common in males.

Diagnoses of ADD and AD/HD among teens and adolescents have more than doubled in the last 15 years, although how much of that is attributable to an increase in the actual condition as opposed to the ability to better diagnose the condition is the subject of continued debate. We believe that this rise is also partly due to the dramatic increase in technology use among children generally, as children who are addicted to technology tend to display many of the symptoms of traditional ADD and/or AD/HD, but may not necessarily actually have ADD or AD/HD. When kids who are addicted to technology—but do *not* have ADD or AD/HD—have their technology taken away, their HD symptoms go away.

As of this writing, research *does* show a link between Attention Deficit Disorders and excessive screen time. However, kids with ADD and AD/HD also have a thinner cerebral cortex and structural differences involving the transport of dopamine, which likely contributes to making them more vulnerable to technology addictions.

How Technology Affects Children with Attention Deficit

Unfortunately for children with a diagnosis of Attention Deficit, the mere act of sitting quietly in school and paying attention can be a struggle, and that struggle can have devastating effects on their long-term academic performance. It is normal for them to struggle in school, as their mind constantly wanders, while AD/HD kids also fidget regularly. Their inattention and inability to focus, combined with a flashy, addictive device buzzing in their pocket, explains the academic difficulties we so typically associate with ADD and AD/HD kids.

However, as with Autism Spectrum Disorders, a diagnosis of ADD or AD/HD is *not* all doom and gloom. Although kids with ADD and AD/HD may generally struggle with inattention, they also possess the unique ability to *hyperfocus* for short periods of time. One acquaintance of ours, for example, is known for his Attention Deficit. In fact, his wife diagnosed him 10 minutes into their first date! But his strong ability to hyperfocus for short bursts of time makes him an excellent emergency room doctor, tasked with saving the lives of people arriving in his care having suffered car accidents, heart attacks, gunshot wounds, etc. in which every second can mean the difference between life and death. Although he's in his element in the emergency room, when he was a resident, his wife told him that she'd divorce him if he ever tried to become a surgeon. Brilliant as he was in the emergency room, he couldn't stand being on his feet in the operating room for 12 hours!

Here again, technology can be your friend. Children with Attention Deficit have issues with time management, organization, and a failure to pay attention to detail, but something as simple as a personal planner or organizational software installed on your children's devices can be a lifesaver, particularly for reminding the ones in adolescence to do their chores, when major school projects are due, or when tryouts are scheduled for a particular sports team or theater production. The challenge for you as a parent is to ensure that your children are using their devices for the right reasons and in the right amounts, rather than spending endless hours playing games. ADD and AD/HD kids' ability to hyperfocus can also cause them to get lost in video games and online behavior even more than most children. Although a typical child may lose an hour playing a video game, a child with Attention Deficit can easily lose 5 hours the same way.

How We Can Manage Technology for Children with Attention Deficit

Luckily for those who have a child with Attention Deficit, the tech industry has also focused heavily on creating sustainable solutions for all of us. For instance, there are apps and computer programs today that can help your child stay organized, manage project goals, schedule their day, etc. to stay on task and pace themselves as they work. Research thus far shows that students with Attention Deficit who use technology apps and programs have increased academic performance, greater self-esteem, and higher confidence in peer interactions—all music to a parent's ears!

Use a Digital Disruption to Separate Technology from the Disorder. One strategy we recommend for parents to disentangle their children's use of technology from a possible diagnosis of AD/HD is to undertake what we call a "digital disruption." Think of it like an addict who enters rehab and then has a "drying out" period. For 30 days, take away your children's iPads, video games, cell phone games, etc. You might allow some television viewing, but only in moderation.

The first week will be hard, full of lots of crying and anger, but we've had numerous families report that this has made a *tremendous* impact on their children's AD/HD symptoms. In mild cases, this has helped to practically erase the child's symptoms, while in moderate to severe cases it can—at a minimum—lessen your child's symptoms.

If you see no change in your child's behavior after 30 days, then you'll know that the technology itself isn't the issue; however, should you see a dramatic change in your child, then you'll know that his or her technology use is the critical variable that's influencing their symptoms, and you should formulate a plan to find that right balance—our Goldilocks Zone—for technology use.

RESOURCES FOR PARENTS WITH CHILDREN WITH ATTENTION DEFICIT

Children and Adults with Attention Deficit/Hyperactivity Disorder (CHADD): provides evidence-based information, support, and public advocacy on ADD or AD/HD issues

ADDvance: British charity unites parents and professionals working on ADD issues

Attention Deficit Disorder Association: provides support for adolescents and adults in transition to work and higher education

ADDitude Magazine: magazine for families about all things ADD or AD/HD

Attention Research Update: newsletter from Duke researcher on ADD or AD/HD research

Other Neurodevelopmental Disorders

Autism Spectrum Disorders and Attention Deficit Disorders are some of the most well-known challenges facing parents today, although they're not the sole problems that parents may face. The DSM clusters together the various challenges that a person may face in childhood—such as Autism Spectrum Disorders and Attention Deficit Disorders—separately from those that may occur at any point in a person's life (depression, anxiety, etc.), or later in the lifespan, such as schizophrenia or Alzheimer's. Much of this boils down to the medical community's efforts to find the best science which differentiates various conditions from each other, so as to understand which symptoms each condition presents, what causes those conditions, how best to treat them, and, if possible, how to prevent them in the future.

As parents, the first sign we might have that something is wrong with our child is that gut feeling that something is "off" with our child, particularly in comparison to other children his or her age. This can take the form of our child's not meeting a particular developmental milestone on time, not being able to perform a certain task the right way, or not reacting to the outside world in a way that we might expect. Those intuitions of ours are a *very* important first step in finding out what's wrong—or simply different—with our child so that we can begin to get him or her the care and the tools that will be needed to succeed in life. Although we'll discuss its downsides later in the chapter, the federal No Child Left Behind Act and its various legal successors (Every Student Succeeds Act, etc.) have done an excellent job of shining a spotlight on the needs of disadvantaged learners in the school system, whether due to a medical condition or the challenges of poverty.

Neurodevelopmental disorders run the course of a person's life, although the symptoms of each particular condition may change over time. The may also vary from child to child—and life stage to life stage—as a result of different culture factors.

For us as parents, these kinds of diagnoses can be utterly devastating, but we have to remember that a diagnosis can also simply mean a *difference*. Like Michael Phelps's long arms, many of today's best rap artists had stutters as children. We can't forget that, despite how well some of us may be at keeping up appearances, there are no perfect people; we all have our struggles.

How Technology Affects Children with Neurodevelopmental Disorders

The first challenge for parents of children with neurodevelopmental issues is to begin to distinguish between technology use and the underlying condition that your child is facing. In some cases, technology can make a condition worse (think of video games causing seizures), while in other situations your children may be liable to lag in their development because they find their particular technology so enticing. Parents need to be mindful of the other recommendations we've outlined in the book and be able to make judgment calls as to whether our more general recommendations will work for their particular child and his or her specific needs. Remember, it's important to avoid the "one size fits all" mentality.

One additional challenge for parents of children with neurodevelopmental issues is to distinguish between their children's chronological (actual physical) age and their developmental age, i.e. their maturity. For example, a child with moderate intellectual disabilities may be 12 years old chronologically but have the intellectual and emotional development of a 5-year-old, requiring parents and educators to create an environment for the child that addresses the discrepancy. In this example, we would recommend leading with the child's intellectual and emotional age rather than his or her chronological age.

How We Can Manage Technology for Children with Neurodevelopmental Disorders

The most important thing that parents can do for their child facing a neurodevelopmental disorder is to learn as much as you can about whatever challenges your child is facing and what the road ahead will be like. Learning as much as you can about the terminology of your child's condition, the symptoms it presents, and the treatment paths available will also help in navigating the school, government, and medical bureaucracies you'll have to fight to get your child the resources and support he or she needs. In contrast, the inexact terminology of technology usage issues means that health insurance companies, hospitals, and medical organizations have to develop something as simple as diagnostic and billing codes to deliver effective care for those problems on an institutional level.

Secondly, particularly when they're younger, we *strongly* recommend that parents of children with neurodevelopmental disorders restrict (or at a minimum, supervise) their child's technology use, because children with these particular issues are much less equipped to deal with the sheer amount of filth in cyberspace nowadays. Although catching your high school child viewing Internet pornography may be annoying, younger children with neurodevelopmental disorders may be shocked and even traumatized by the experience of seeing hardcore pornography or the violence of today's video games, and they can even be radicalized by extremist groups from all across the political spectrum. The sheer damage that this material can do to an unknowing child is a key driver behind the efforts of many parent groups today to clean up cyberspace. Until you have a good diagnosis of your child's condition and roadmap for treatment, it's better to err on the side of caution with your child's technology use.

Thirdly, we also recommend connecting with local support groups and chapters of the organizations that represent your child's unique needs. This will allow you to network with other parents and share best practices as well as find out what treatment options and support programs are available for your family both locally and nationally. Remember: you are *not* alone!

PARENT RESOURCES FOR CHILDREN
WITH NEURODEVELOPMENTAL DISORDERS

The Arc: national organization provides support services and advocacy for individuals and families with intellectual and developmental disabilities

Healthy Communication and Popular Technology Initiative: provides resources for parents and educators from American Speech-Language-Hearing Association

National Center for Learning Disabilities: provides lifelong support and resources for individuals and families with learning disabilities

Dyspraxia Foundation USA: provides resources and referrals for motor disorders

Tourette Association of America: provides awareness, research, and support for individuals with Tourette Syndrome and other tic disorders

Administration on Intellectual and Developmental Disabilities: federal agency funds numerous state and local grant programs for various disability programs

Parenting Special Needs Magazine: bi-monthly magazine and website with resources

Strategies for Managing Technology
for Children with Unique Needs

Make Technology Your Friend

Once you've educated yourself about your particular child's challenges, we strongly recommend finding the ways that you can use technology to educate your child about the broader world. Many of the national organizations we mention in this chapter are now publishing lists of recommended apps and other technologies that you can access with little cost or—because they are recommended by national organizations—may be covered by your health insurance. Finding that right piece of technology for a unique needs child at the right age can potentially change that child's life for the better. A good time management app can be a godsend for an AD/HD child, for example.

Never Hand New Technology to Your Kids
Without Learning It First

One important consideration for children with unique needs is that they may not necessarily respond to the stimulus offered by technology in ways that it was designed for. Tech engineers are both human and have to cater to a general audience, so there's always an outside chance that your child will react inappropriately or be hurt emotionally by an encounter with technology. As with the nutrition labels on food, we strongly suggest taking the product warnings and online reviews for toys, games, phones, etc. seriously before letting a child with unique needs use the product. This again is where you have to be the parent rather than a friend to your children, no matter how many temper tantrums they may throw in front of you.

Get a Second Opinion

Remember that doctors are people too. Different doctors will have different approaches and philosophies, meaning that your neighborhood family physician may not be the best doctor to treat your child. If you don't like what you're hearing, find another doctor—particularly one tied into a university, research hospital, or teaching hospital, who is more likely to be most up to date on the best practices in treating your child's issues.

Don't Let a Google Search Define Your Child

While the information available online and books like this are always a good start, don't make them the be-all, end-all for information about your child. One of the most dangerous elements of labeling a child is that from an early age, we then operate with preconceived notions about what our child is and isn't capable of. Those mental boxes are some of the most detrimental things we as parents can operate with.

Know Your Rights

As you network with other parents, one ongoing challenge will be having to work with your local school system to ensure that your kids get the education that they deserve, and which they are legally entitled to.

COMMON EDUCATIONAL INTERVENTION PROGRAMS

Individualized Education Program (IEP): custom academic plan for special needs children, mandated by law and to be provided in the least restrictive environment.

Behavior Intervention Plan (BIP): custom plan for students with behavior issues, with appropriate punishments and rewards. Should address the child's underlying problems rather than any superficial needs, such as a child's acting out because of a pending divorce.

504 Plan: custom plan to ensure equal access to school services for students not requiring specialized instruction, such as wheelchair ramps or help taking notes in class.

KEY TAKEAWAYS FROM THIS CHAPTER

- There's no such thing as a normal child.

- The diversity of the natural world includes different designs of the human brain.

- Effective mental health treatment requires understanding a person's biology, psychology, and sociology.

- Technology use affects the brains of children with neurodevelopmental disorders in different, unique ways that require us to learn all we can about our children's issues to find which practices work best for them and which don't.

- The tech industry is rising to the challenge to provide instructional and developmental tools for parents and children, but more research needs to be done.

ACTION STEPS

- Know your kids, trust yourself, and educate yourself about your child's issues.

- Focus on *how* your kids are intelligent, not *whether* they are intelligent.

- Learn about your children's technology before you give it to them.

- Use the resources of the book.

- Be patient, and don't forget to take care of yourself.

FOR FURTHER READING

- *The End of Average: Unlocking Our Potential by Embracing What Makes Us Different*, by Todd Rose

- *The Autistic Brain*, by Dr. Temple Grandin

- *Ten Things Every Child With Autism Wishes You Knew*, by Ellen Notbohm

- *Driven to Distraction: Recognizing and Coping with Attention Deficit Disorder from Childhood Through Adulthood*, by Edward M. Hallowell and John J. Ratey

SECTION FOUR
There Is Hope

CHAPTER FOURTEEN

Mistakes Happen

---

*"I have not failed.
I've just found 10,000 ways that won't work."*
—THOMAS EDISON

Mistakes Are Part of the Process

Being the adult in the room can be a humbling process, as we often don't feel like adults ourselves until our 30s, and many of us have children before hitting that milestone and feeling comfortable in the adult world. We *will* make mistakes along the way, but the important thing is that we don't make the same mistake twice. Hopefully you will learn from our experiences and from the best practices available today, but as we all know, some children just have to get their fingers burned on the hot stove, no matter what you tell them. We all make mistakes, but the important thing to remember is that odds are good that most of your mistakes—including the ones you don't even know you're making—probably won't be life threatening. The key is to get better with time, as parenting your children will become easier with experience.

Know Your Kids and Trust Yourself

Although knowing your kids almost goes without saying, you're going to know your children better than a professional who's meeting them for the first time. More often than not, your gut intuition about your children *will* be right. Remember, every child is a bit different and "normal" doesn't really exist. That puts the burden on you as the parent and caretaker to help guide your children through their developmental challenges.

There is only so much depth that we can provide in a book on the general issues of technology overuse and addiction, which is why as a parent you should supplement our advice by reading everything you can about whatever particular issues are facing your children. We encourage you to accept that you may make a mistake, but that's okay we have made them too.

Minimizing Mistakes

Never Hand New Technology to Your Kids Without Learning It First

One important consideration for children is that they may not necessarily respond to the stimulus offered by technology in ways that it was designed for. Tech engineers are hired to develop programs that cater to a general audience and retain users not necessarily to ensure the safety of your children, so there's always an outside chance that your child may be hurt emotionally by an encounter using technology. As with the nutrition labels on food, we strongly suggest taking the product warnings and online reviews for toys, games, phones, etc. seriously before giving your child access. This again is where you have to be the parent rather than a friend to your children, no matter how many temper tantrums they may throw in front of you.

Let Your Child Teach You the Technology

Once you've done your homework about whatever technology you put in your child's hands, a good bonding experience for the two of you will be for you to let your child teach it to you. This will also allow you as the digital immigrant to let your child, the digital native, teach you some of the nuances as to how the particular piece of technology works and doesn't work. As the adult in the room, you'll be able to then figure out on a more detailed level how to help customize the technology for your child to help his or her developmental needs, and to then share those best practices with other parents and your child's teachers.

Focus on Quality over Quantity

Depending on the technology, your child's neurological wiring may leave him or her vulnerable to the addictive designs of today's technology, making it that much easier for them to spend endless hours connected to a particular device, playing a particular game, etc. It's particularly important that you steer them *away* from the devices or programs they *shouldn't* be using (much, if at all) and *towards* the devices and programs they *should* be using.

Use the Resources in the Book

You are not alone in trying to raise a happy, healthy child, regardless of whatever challenges you face. The national organizations we list throughout this book will all be invaluable resources to find best practices with technology and to connect with other parents facing those same issues.

Be Patient and Forgive Yourself

Many of the situations that we outline in this book are based on real life incidents. In the end, this is not easy work and trying to understand the digital world and it's influences on your child takes great patience and a profound sense of humility. Remember to forgive yourself for the mistakes you will inevitably make. No one is perfect, and although we all try to be the best parents we can, we will get things wrong. Our kids will let us know it of course, and we'll get the glare from other parents, but no one is perfect.

CHAPTER FIFTEEN

The Case for Optimism

"Parenthood is about raising and celebrating the child you have,
not the child you thought you'd have. It's about understanding that
your child is exactly the person they are supposed to be.
And, if you're lucky, they might be the teacher who turns you
into the person you're supposed to be."

—JOAN RYAN in *The Water Giver*

The Tide is Turning

The first step in solving any problem is to acknowledge that there is one. The fact that you're reading this book—and we're writing it—tells all of us that this issue will get solved. We may not all agree on the details, but we can agree that this is a problem that needs to get solved.

Think back to the metaphor of the Industrial Revolution. All over the world, in the short (by historical standards) period of a few decades, nearly every facet of human existence was completely transformed. Despite the rapid changes brought on after 9/11 with TSA and the restrictions from the pandemic brought on by Covid-19, we managed to survive, with our humanity intact. We will get through this, but with plenty of creative destruction along the way.

There are always moments of despair in which we think that all is lost, and yet somehow later on, people manage to pull through and move on to brighter and better days. This too will happen with your children and their inability to look up from their screens. It may take a few lawsuits—this is America, of course—and more than a bit of reform, regulation, and redesign, but it will happen. The discussions in the news media and the conversations you have with other parents at PTO/PTA meetings are turning the tide on this. We know that this needs to change, and any time we have casual conversations with parents about this subject, a nod of agreement is the first response they all have. Things may not always turn out exactly as we'd have liked, but they will work themselves out over time.

Give Your Kids the Tools and They'll Make the Right Decision

The most inspiring part of our work with kids and technology issues is that when we present them with the right tools and the right information, they typically make the right decisions. Our kids should know by now that the things they say online can't be erased, and that cruel words can hurt others, but when we present them with the full picture of *how* those words and actions affect others, the positive changes in online behavior can be dramatic. Once kids understand the big picture, they can begin to restrain themselves and police each other without nearly as much interference (as they see it) from adults. This is all the more important considering that we adults will always be at least one step behind our kids on technology issues. In the same way that kids never tell us about the worst things that happen to them in the locker room or at a scouting campout, so too will they not tell us about the things that happen to them online.

Think of this book as an additional set of tools, based upon both rigorous research and our own clinical experience with best practices, as a way for you to begin to empower your children to make those good decisions when you won't be there. Much as it can be difficult to imagine when our kids are younger, there *will* be a day when we can't be there, when teachers, coaches, and other trusted adults can't be there, and our children will have to make their own decisions—about drugs, about dating, about sex, about marriage, about jobs and careers, etc. All the more important to teach our children to do the right thing when they're young.

One of our challenges in developing good science around issues of technology overuse and addiction is separating the normal ups and downs of childhood from the new wrinkle of being connected 24/7 to technology. Children have always had issues learning to navigate the world, and we now have the neurological research to understand why. Raising children has never been easy, but as parents we're fortunate to have more tools than any previous generation. That doesn't make things easy when your child is throwing a temper tantrum the night before your major presentation at work, but it does make things easier for you than it was for your parents.

Start Young

> "It is easier to build strong children than to repair broken men."
> —FREDERICK DOUGLASS

We mentioned generational differences at the outset of the book because that's one key underlying factor in understanding our children's relationship with technology today. They're simply growing up differently than we grew up, or our parents grew up, or their own children will one day grow up. The pace of change continues to accelerate, and that's why so much of our parting advice here is proactive rather than reactive. Remember, your children need you as a *parent* and not as a *friend*. If you do your job as a parent, the friend part will come later. It's infinitely easier to establish rules with your children when they're young than to try and pivot backwards and start once they've hit junior high and high school.

Be In It for the Long Haul

A parent's work is never done, and so long as we have children, we will *always* be their parents. The relationship may evolve over time (your children won't always be children) but the dynamic will *always* be the same. One friend of ours tells a story of visiting his 95-year-old grandmother in the nursing home with his adult parents, only to see his 95-year-old grandmother correct his 65-year-old father—not exactly a child—in front of everyone. Upon leaving the nursing home, our friend remarked to his father, "I guess that never changes." No, it doesn't.

The changes facing you and your friends in this generation of parents will be different from those faced by your own parents, and from those your children will face when they have children of their own. The only constant in life is change, but that parental intuition and gut instinct, backed by lots of sound research, will help all of us raise another generation of happy, healthy, prosperous children. When pressed to admit it, our parents will even tell us that they made more than their share of mistakes, too.

CHAPTER SIXTEEN

Making Memories

"There are no perfect parents and there are no perfect children, but there are plenty of perfect moments along the way."
—DAVE WILLIS

They'll Be Out of the House Before You Know It

Last but not least, it's important to remember that your children will be children for only so long before they're launched off into adulthood. Some may choose to settle in another city or even another country, and today we all know that "talking" with someone over Zoom is not the same thing as a genuine face-to-face conversation. Time and distance create a space in relationships that's hard to fill with visits no matter how long or short they are.

10 IDEAS TO CREATE MEANINGFUL FAMILY MOMENTS

- Plant a family garden
- Plan a family vacation together
- Conduct family interviews
- Cook and eat a family meal
- Take a family nature walk
- Designate a family holiday
- Host a family sports event

- Have a family movie of the week

- Start a family book club
- Make family art

Source: *Parents* magazine

So be sure to treasure those moments with your children. The days may indeed be long, but the years are painfully short, and they will be over before you know it.

Say No to Tech, and Yes to Making Some Memories

As we've discussed throughout the book, saying yes to technology often means that kids are neglecting other aspects of their development. In the short term, it may be easy for us to dump our kids in front of the video game or tablet so we can get some work done, but in the long run, we all know that that isn't healthy.

Although it takes some work to implement the steps we've outlined in this book, you'll see, although it may not be easy, it will *definitely* be worth it. One nugget we came across in writing this book was that parents have only 940 Saturdays from the time their children are born to the time the kids leave for college, career, and other post-secondary plans. Although the days may seem long at times, the years themselves are definitely short.... So all the more important to make the best of every one of them. Our kids only get one childhood, and we only get one shot at raising them, so best that we make it count. We—and society as a whole—have to live with the results.

Don't Confuse Making a Living with Making a Life

One message that's been lost in our culture in recent generations is the difference between working and living. Europeans, it's said, work to live, while Americans live to work. That's certainly true in our big cities and especially on the coasts, where long hours and work emails after midnight are common. But while delivering results for clients may be great for generating income, it's not the same thing as building a life for yourself and for your family. Most of the research in psychology in recent decades has found that above an annual income of around $75,000 (translation: enough to satisfy most material desires), money has no effect on happiness.

COMMON END OF LIFE REGRETS

- I wish I lived for myself more
- I wish I didn't work so hard
- I wish I didn't hold back my feelings
- I wish I stayed in touch
- I wish I cared less of what others think

- I wish I was happier
- I wish I didn't worry so much
- I wish I took better care of myself
- I wish I didn't take life for granted
- I wish I lived in the now

Sources: Australian palliative care nurse Bronnie Ware, PowerOfPositivity.com

It's always tempting for us to answer that late night call from a colleague, to say yes to a project at work, or to say yes to an organization that needs our expertise, but saying yes to those professional and community responsibilities also means that we're saying no to our children. The difference is that while there will always be more work that needs to be done at our jobs and in our communities, we only get that one shot to raise our kids. Each of our kids will only be 6 years old or 12 years old once and with each of those years comes a unique set of challenges and opportunities for us as parents that we'll never get back. Meanwhile, the work will continue to pile up elsewhere regardless of our individual contributions.

How Does A Child Spell Love? T-i-m-e

"Children begin by loving their parents; as they grow older
they judge them; sometimes they forgive them."
—OSCAR WILDE

In addition to the basic salary issue—how much money is enough—psychological research in recent decades has found that we generate more happiness by spending money on experiences rather than on things. As we all know from watching kids opening up holiday presents, once the desire for the new toy is over, the toy is soon discarded and our kids are off craving the next shiny object (and the most fun, satisfying toy is often the cardboard box for a new refrigerator). Adaptation generally means that we acclimate to our material circumstances, whatever they are. Material prosperity and happiness are only loosely correlated worldwide, and despite what the advertisements say—he who dies with the most toys... still dies.

This is why the onus is on us as parents and caretakers to make sure that we spend quality *time* with our children. It's not an accident that so many of our suggestions centered on shared *experiences* with our children; while buying them things may temporarily assuage our guilt, those aren't the things that our children will remember. What they *will* remember are the times that we spent with them at museums, at the zoo, or when we spent time listening to their concerns, no matter how petty they might seem to us at the time. If you think back to your own childhood, odds are good that some of your happiest memories are the times that you spent doing things with your parents or your siblings, rather than acquiring the latest and greatest toy.

Take Care of Yourself

"Your time is limited, so don't waste it living someone else's life ... Don't let the noise of others' opinions drown out your own inner voice. And most important, have the courage to follow your heart and intuition. They somehow already know what you truly want to become. Everything else is secondary."
—STEVE JOBS, 2005 Stanford commencement speech

You have to take care of yourself, which is hard since we're often so busy taking care of other people that we forget to take care of ourselves. Whenever you're tired, stressed, being pulled in multiple directions, etc., and you can't be there for your children, your job, your partner, your elderly parents, etc., *there's nothing wrong with taking care of yourself.* Giving yourself permission to put aside your responsibilities for a brief respite isn't wrong, and will make you a better parent, spouse, caregiver, and employee over the long term.

Keep in mind that your children will learn far more from your *example* than they will from anything you ever say. Actions speak louder than words, and if your children only ever see you tired and stressed, then they'll internalize that as normal in their own lives.

Sometimes taking care of yourself means saying "no." Billionaire investor Warren Buffett famously says no to 95% of the proposals that come across his desk. The reason is not because a large percentage of those proposals are somehow lacking, but because he wants to be able to focus on the 5% of projects that come his way and which he can *fully* engage in. Saying yes to one thing means saying no to other things, and that forces us all to choose our priorities—saying yes to your job and yes to your kids means that you'll have to pass on a bowling league or a sewing club, no matter how much you might enjoy those other activities.

This is all easier said than done, of course, when we have work, family, friends, and the responsibility to put nutritious food in our kids' bellies and help with homework they don't understand. Happiness must be defined by small successes, however you might define them, having supportive friends that commiserate with your mistakes, family that will be there in good times and bad, and most importantly, kids that become good humans.

Epilogue

"You've got to be careful if you don't know where you're going,
because you might not get there."

—YOGI BERRA

IF THERE'S ANY LESSON THAT WE'VE LEARNED IN REFLECTING upon our experiences, researching, and writing this book, it's that changes in technology are evolving at an exponential pace. Current changes include: citizens in Sweden having microchips injected underneath their skin to serve as permanent identification and remove the need for such things as passports, driver's licenses, and credit cards; electric driverless cars are being introduced as concept cars in France; and China is installing a "social credit" system which combines security cameras, facial recognition technology, and big data to monitor the behavior of 1.4 billion people, providing perks for those who comport themselves well, along with heavy restrictions on those whom the government considers a threat to public safety. Meanwhile, IBM's supercomputers have beaten the world's best human beings at chess and Jeopardy, with academic debate competition as the next benchmark in the evolution of artificial intelligence.

These things are happening now. Not 50 years from now, but *right now*.

Our parting advice, as both parents and professionals who have sifted through reams of the latest research along with our own experience in clinical practices and preparing presentations for various professional conferences, is to do the best you can to *prepare your children for a world that is constantly changing.*

Give yourself credit for doing the best that you can. You *will* make mistakes, as *none* of us are perfect and *every* generation has its own unique challenges. We'll get through this—just as soon as your kids put down their devices and do their homework, of course. Parenting isn't easy for anyone, and even though this is our area of expertise, we've had our own arguments, celebrations, and realizations along the way even while writing this book. Don't give up, don't be afraid to ask questions, and don't worry if you have to change lanes or turn around, pivot, and do something different. Our kids push boundaries just like yours do, they get angry about limits, they challenge every decision we make, and they can make us question sometimes whether the ends justify the means. We talk to friends, read the research, and try to find the right balancing act just like you do. We too are Goldilocks trying to find that Zone. It isn't easy, but... it's worth it.

Appendix

Self-Reporting Children's Screening Tool

☐ Do you spend more than two hours per day, outside of schoolwork, using your computer, tablet, or cell phone?

☐ Did you meet more than half of your friends online?

☐ Do your parents repeatedly ask you to top using your computer, tablet, or cell phone, but you can't stop?

☐ To avoid problems with your parents, do you use your computer, tablet, or cell phone late at night after they have gone to bed?

☐ Have you been feeling depressed or particularly moody within the last several months?

☐ Have you lost any or some of your friends because they no longer understand you?

☐ Do you get less than eight hours of sleep, four or more nights per week?

If you answered yes to at least two of the above items, you are at risk of overusing technology.

TUC–Elementary School Children

Behavioral Symptoms and Development

☐ Does your child argue with you about turning off technology or violate limits you have established for technology use in your house?

☐ Do you feel like your child is asking to use technology more often than before?

☐ Have you implemented rules or guidelines about technology use?

☐ Have you had any teachers or administrators report your child has behavior or attention problems during the school day?

☐ Does your child prefer to engage in technology over sports, music, or peer play?

☐ Have you had any conflict related to technology within the family (e.g., arguments, storming off, tantrums, crying, etc.)?

If you answered yes to at least three items your child is at risk of overusing technology.

Physical Symptoms and Development

☐ Does your child appear tired (e.g., lacks energy, frequently yawns , etc.)?

☐ Do you have problems getting your child to engage in 60 minutes of physical activity every day?

☐ Do you have concerns about your child's weight (either overweight or underweight)?

☐ Do you notice your child squinting or straining to look at things?

If you answered yes to at least two items your child is at risk of overusing technology.

Emotional Symptoms and Development

- ☐ Do you feel your child demonstrates periods of unusual sadness or outbursts of anger?

- ☐ Would you describe your child as anxious (worries or anticipates next steps, has stomach complaints or headaches)?

- ☐ Does your child demonstrate rage or extreme anger when technology is taken away?

- ☐ Does your child's mood improve when engaged in technology?

If you answered yes to two items or yes to item 8 your child is at risk of overusing technology.

Interpersonal Symptoms and Development

- ☐ Does your child have trouble maintaining good interpersonal skills during conversations (e.g., good eye contact, appropriate nonverbal skills, speaks clearly or with enough volume)?

- ☐ Does your child prefer to watch or play video games with friends over playing any other activity with friends?

- ☐ Does your child have difficulty making friends?

- ☐ Does your child have trouble resolving conflicts and accepting conflict resolution appropriately?

- ☐ Does your child fail to use an appropriate amount of assertiveness to communicate needs, desires, beliefs, and ideas with others?

If you answered yes to two items or at least yes to item 2 your child is at risk of overusing technology.

TUC–Teens

Behavioral Health

☐ Does your child have a hard time stopping their use of technology when requested?

☐ Does your child spend increasing amounts of time using technology?

☐ Have you made unsuccessful attempts to limit your child's technology use?

☐ Has your child's school performance become problematic (e.g., incomplete homework, failing on tests, or sleeping through class)?

☐ Has your child given up previously enjoyed hobbies (e.g., sports, dramatics, music, outdoor recreation)?

☐ Does your child's use of technology cause arguments in your family?

If you answered yes to at least three items your child is at risk of overusing technology.

Physical Health

☐ Does your child appear tired (e.g., dark circles or blood shot eyes, lacks energy, frequently yawns, etc.)?

☐ Is it hard to get your child to engage in physical activities for at least 60 minutes a day?

☐ Does your child consume energy drinks or other caffeinated drinks?

☐ Do you notice your child squinting or straining to look at things?

☐ Does your child complain of upper body discomfort (e.g., hands, wrists, back or shoulders)?

☐ Does your child have poor grooming habits (showers, nail care, dental hygiene)?

If you answered yes to at least three items your child is at risk of overusing technology.

Emotional Health

☐ Does your child demonstrate periods of unusual sadness or anger?

☐ Does your child seem to be emotionally withdrawn?

☐ Does your child demonstrate periods of unusual anxiety (e.g., nervousness or worry)?

☐ Does your child's mood improve when engaged in technology?

☐ Does your child demonstrate rage or extreme anger when technology is taken away?

☐ Does your child demonstrate dramatic mood swings?

If you answered yes to three items or yes to item 17 your child is at risk of overusing technology.

Interpersonal Health

☐ Do you feel as though you don't know any of your child's friends?

☐ Does your child have poor interpersonal skills during conversations (poor eye contact, awkward nonverbal skills, hard to hear speech)?

☐ Does your child spend increasing amounts of time alone or prefer to be alone?

☐ Are most of your child's friends online friends?

☐ Do your child's conversations with friends primarily occur via text, chat, or instant message?

☐ Does your child become irate, irritable, or anxious during periods when he or she does not have access to electronic device (e.g., during meals, family functions, appointments, etc.)?

If you answered yes to three items or yes to item 22 or item 24 your child is at risk of overusing technology.

Self-Reporting Adult Screening Tool

☐ Do you spend more than two hours per day, outside of work or school, using your computer, tablet, or cell phone?

☐ Is your computer, tablet, or cell phone the first thing you look at in the morning or the last thing you look at before you go to bed, four or more days per week?

☐ Have your children asked you to stop using your computer, tablet, or cell phone on more than a couple of occasions?

☐ Do you check email, messages, or take phone calls while eating a meal with your family?

☐ Have you engaged in risky behavior online that your family, spouse, or significant other would not approve of?

If you answered yes to two or more items above you are at risk of overusing technology.

Notes

PREFACE

Anderson, M., & Jiang, J. (2018). *"Teens, Social Media & Technology 2018"* (White Paper). Pew Research Center, Washington, DC. Retrieved from https://www.pewinternet.org/2018/05/31/teens-social-media-technology-2018/

Rasmussen Reports. (2018, June). *"Half Think Their Fellow Americans Play Video Games Too Much."* Retrieved from http://www.rasmussenreports.com/public_content/lifestyle/general_lifestyle/june_2018/half_think_their_fellow_americans_play_video_games_too_much

Rasmussen Reports. (2017, September). *Americans Still See Too Much Screen Time for Kids*. Retrieved from http://www.rasmussenreports.com/public_content/lifestyle/general_lifestyle/september_2017/americans_still_see_too_much_screen_time_for_kids

Natanson, H. (2017, June 5). Harvard Rescinds Acceptances for At Least Ten Students for Obscene Memes. *Harvard Crimson*. Retrieved from https://www.thecrimson.com/article/2017/6/5/2021-offers-rescinded-memes/

McKewon, S. (2018, June 20). Recruits, be warned. Husker Coach Scott Frost is watching your social media. *Omaha World-Herald*. Retrieved from https://www.omaha.com/huskers/football/recruiting/recruits-be-warned-husker-coach-scott-frost-is-watching-your/article_673ad077-22fa-5aa6-a935-72737de286e9.html

CHAPTER ONE: LIFE IN THE 21ST CENTURY

Luntz, F.I. (2009). *What Americans Really Want… Really*. New York, NY: Hyperion.

Common Sense Media. (2016). *"Technology Addiction: Concern, Controversy, and Finding Balance"* (White Paper). Retrieved from https://www.commonsensemedia.org/sites/default/files/uploads/research/csm_2016_technology_addiction_research_brief_0.pdf

American Psychiatry Association. (2018, June). "Internet Gaming." Retrieved from https://www.psychiatry.org/patients-families/internet-gaming

Notes

American Academy of Pediatrics. (2016, October 21). "*American Academy of Pediatrics Announces New Recommendations for Children's Media Use.*" Retrieved from https://www.aap.org/en-us/about-the-aap/aap-press-room/pages/american-academy-of-pediatrics-announces-new-recommendations-for-childrens-media-use.aspx

Anderson, M., & Jiang, J. (2018). "*Teens, Social Media & Technology 2018*" (White Paper). Pew Research Center, Washington, DC. Retrieved from https://www.pewinternet.org/2018/05/31/teens-social-media-technology-2018/

CHAPTER TWO: INTRODUCING GENERATION Z

McBride, T., Nief, R., & Westerberg, C. (2018, August 20). *The Mindset List: Class of 2022.* Retrieved from http://themindsetlist.com/2018/08/beloit-college-mindset-list-class-2022/

Pew Research Center. (2015). *Parenting in America* (White Paper). Washington, DC. Retrieved from https://www.pewsocialtrends.org/2015/12/17/parenting-in-america/

Iqbal, N. (2018, July 21). "Generation Z: 'We have more to do than drink and take drugs.'" *The Guardian.* Retrieved from https://www.theguardian.com/society/2018/jul/21/generation-z-has-different-attitudes-says-a-new-report

Oxford Royale Academy. (2018, January 25). *7 Unique Characteristics of Generation Z.* Retrieved from https://www.oxford-royale.com/articles/7-unique-characteristics-generation-z.html

Ryan, C. (2018, August 8). *Computer and Internet Use in the United States: 2016.* United States Census Bureau. Retrieved from https://www.census.gov/library/publications/2018/acs/acs-39.html

Elmore, T. (2017, September 28). 6 Terms That Summarize Generation Z's Mindset. *Psychology Today.* Retrieved from https://www.psychologytoday.com/us/blog/artificial-maturity/201709/6-terms-summarize-generation-z-s-mindset

Pew Research Center. (2015). *Parenting in America* (White Paper). Washington, DC. Retrieved from https://www.pewsocialtrends.org/2015/12/17/parenting-in-america/

Twenge, J.M. & Park, H. (2019, March/April). The Decline in Adult Activities Among U.S. Adolescents, 1976-2016. *Child Development, 90,* 638-654. DOI: 10.1111/cdev.12930

Notes

Vespa, J. (2017, April). *The Changing Economics and Demographics of Young Adulthood: 1975-2016*. United States Census Bureau. Retrieved from https://www.census.gov/library/publications/2017/demo/p20-579.html

CHAPTER THREE: THE DEVELOPING BRAIN

Wnuk, A. (2015, April 9). Brain Evolution: Searching for What Makes Us Human. Society for Neuroscience. Retrieved from https://www.brainfacts.org/brain-anatomy-and-function/evolution/2015/brain-evolution-searching-for-what-makes-us-human

Society for Neuroscience. (2018). *Brain Facts: A Primer on the Brain and Nervous System*. Washington, DC. Retrieved from https://www.brainfacts.org/the-brain-facts-book

Alban, Deane. (2017, September 29). *72 Amazing Human Brain Facts (Based on the Latest Science)*. Retrieved from https://bebrainfit.com/human-brain-facts/

Science First. (n.d.) *10 Interesting Facts about the Human Brain*. Retrieved from https://sciencefirst.com/10-interesting-facts-about-the-human-brain/

F., I. (2018). *Difference Between Grey Matter and White Matter*. Retrieved from http://www.differencebetween.net/science/health/difference-between-grey-and-white-matter/

Laliberte, M. (2019). Brain Development: 10 Ways Your Brain Changes as You Get Older. *Reader's Digest*. Retrieved from https://www.rd.com/health/wellness/brain-development/

Family Development Resources. (2011). *Brain Development; Ages and Stages; Comfort and Calming*. Retrieved from https://www.NurturingParenting.com

Cherry, K. (2018). *When Do Your Mental Powers Peak?* Retrieved from https://www.verywellmind.com/when-do-your-mental-powers-peak-2795033

Wollett, K. & Maguire, E.A. (2011, December 20). Acquiring "the Knowledge" of London's Layout Drives Structural Brain Changes. *Current Biology, 21*, 2109-2114.

Kinderman. P. (2015, March 6). Mental health is a complex, interactive dance of nature and nurture. *The Conversation*. Retrieved from https://theconversation.com/mental-health-is-a-complex-interactive-dance-of-nature-and-nurture-38003

Notes

Harvard University Center on the Developing Child. (2019). *8 Things to Remember About Child Development.* Retrieved from https://developingchild.harvard.edu/resources/8-things-remember-child-development/

CHAPTER FOUR: PROCESS ADDICTIONS AND THE BRAIN

Schmidt, C., Skandali, N., Gleesborg, C. *et al.* (2020) The role of dopaminergic and serotonergic transmission in the processing of primary and monetary reward. *Neuropsychopharmacol.*45, 1490–1497.

Alexander, B.K., Beyerstein, B.L., Hadaway, P.F., & Coambs, R.B. (1981, October). Effect of Early and Later Colony Housing on Oral Ingestion of Morphine in Rats. *Pharmacology, Biochemistry, and Behavior, 15,* 571-576.

Caspani, G, Sebők, V, Sultana, N, Swann, JR, Bailey, A. (2021) Metabolic phenotyping of opioid and psychostimulant addiction: A novel approach for biomarker discovery and biochemical understanding of the disorder. *Br J Pharmacol.* 2021. Accepted Author Manuscript.

Perez, O.D. Instrumental behavior in humans is sensitive to the correlation between response rate and reward rate. (2021) *Psychon Bull Rev* 28, 649–656.

Twine, J., & Williams, J. (2020). The Contextual Effects of Cell Phone Use on Students.

CHAPTER FIVE: TOOLS FOR MANAGING YOUR CHILD'S TECHNOLOGY USE

Harvard Health Letter. (2018, August 13). Blue Light Has a Dark Side. Retrieved from https://www.health.harvard.edu/staying-healthy/blue-light-has-a-dark-side

National Sleep Foundation . (2019). Melatonin and Sleep. Retrieved from https://www.sleepfoundation.org/articles/melatonin-and-sleep

American Academy of Pediatrics. (2016, October 16). *American Academy of Pediatrics Announces New Recommendations for Children's Media Use.* Retrieved from https://www.aap.org/en-us/about-the-aap/aap-press-room/Pages/American-Academy-of-Pediatrics-Announces-New-Recommendations-for-Childrens-Media-Use.aspx

Notes

CHAPTERS SIX, SEVEN, EIGHT, AND NINE: BEHAVIORAL, PHYSICAL, EMOTIONAL, AND INTERPERSONAL FACTORS

Ahmad M, Ahmad U, Fazal Ur Rehman, Khalid Z, Ahmad S. Musculoskeletal neck pain among children and adolescents; Risk factors and complications. Professional Med J 2020; 27(2), 371-376

Layan Al Tawil, Sara Aldokhayel, Leena Zeitouni, Tala Qadoumi, Siham Hussein, Shaik Shaffi Ahamed. Prevalence of self-reported computer vision syndrome symptoms and its associated factors among university students. European Journal of Ophthalmology. 2020; 30(1), 189-195.

Temple, J. L., Bernard, C., Lipshultz, S. E., Czachor, J. D., Westphal, J. A., & Mestre, M. A. (2017). The safety of ingested caffeine: A comprehensive review. Retrieved from https://www.frontiersin.org/articles/10.3389/fpsyt.2017.00080/full

Hirschkowitz, M., et al. (2015, December). National Sleep Foundation's updated sleep duration recommendations: final report. Sleep Health, 1, 233-243.

Children's Hospital of Orange County. (2019). 9 Signs Your Child May Be Considering Suicide. Retrieved from https://www.choc.org/articles/9-signs-your-chil d-may-be-considering-suicide/

Retrieved from https://www.therecoveryvillage.com/mental-health/self-harm/related/ self-harm-statistics/ on 09/29/2020.

Wang, J., Sheng, J., & Wang, H. (2019). The association between mobile game addiction and depression, social anxiety, and loneliness. Retrieved from https://www. frontiersin.org/articles/10.3389/fpubh.2019.00247/full

CHAPTER TEN: VIDEO GAMES

Entertainment Software Association (2018). Essential Facts About the Computer and Video Game Industry. Retrieved from https://www.theesa.com/esa-researc h/2018-essential-facts-about-the-computer-and-video-game-industry/

Palaus, M., Marron, E. M., Viejo-Sobera, R., Redolar-Ripoll, D. (2017) Neural basis of video gaming: A systematic review. Retrieved from https://www.ncbi.nlm.nih.gov/ pmc/articles/PMC5438999/

Notes

Bromberg-Martin, E. S., Matsumoto, M., & Hikosaka, O. (2010). Dopamine in motivational control: rewarding, aversive, and alerting. Retrieved from https://www.ncbi.nlm.nih.gov/pmc/articles/PMC3032992/

Prescott, A. T., Sargent, J. D., & Hull, J. G. (2018). Meta analysis of the relationship between violent video game play and physical aggression over time. Retrieved from https://www.pnas.org/content/115/40/9882

Entertainment Software Rating Board (2019). Retrieved from https://www.esrb.org/ratings-guide/

CHAPTER ELEVEN: PORNOGRAPHY

Guaglione, S. (2018, September 12). "'Playboy' to Become a Quarterly Publication in 2019." *Publishers Daily*. Retrieved from https://www.mediapost.com/publications/article/324818/playboy-to-become-a-quarterly-publication-in-201.html

Fight The New Drug. (2019, January 3). *"20 Mind-Blowing Stats About the Porn Industry And Its Underage Consumers."* Retrieved from https://fightthenewdrug.org/10-porn-stats-that-will-blow-your-mind/

Strange But True. (2017). "How Big is the Porn Industry?" Retrieved from https://medium.com/@Strange_bt_True/how-big-is-the-porn-industry-fbc1ac78091b

EnoughIsEnough. (2019). *"Pornography."* Retrieved from https://enough.org/stats_porn_industry

Dedmon, J. (2002). *"Is the Internet Bad for Your Marriage? Online Affairs, Pornographic Sites Playing Greater Role in Divorces."* American Academy of Matrimonial Lawyers.

Braun-Courville, D.K. and Rojas, M. (2009). "Exposure to Sexually Explicit Web Sites and Adolescent Sexual Attitudes and Behaviors." *Journal of Adolescent Health, 45,* 156-162.

CHAPTER TWELVE: SOCIAL MEDIA AND CYBERBULLYING

Anderson, M., & Jiang, J. (2018). *"Teens, Social Media & Technology 2018"* (White Paper). Pew Research Center, Washington, DC. Retrieved from https://www.pewinternet.org/2018/05/31/teens-social-media-technology-2018/

Wood, A. (2019, March 7). "10 Reasons Middle Schoolers Don't Need Social Media." *FaithIt.com*. Retrieved from https://faithit.com/10-reasons-middle-schoolers-dont-need-social-media-adrian-wood/

Dunckley, V.L. (2017, March 26). "Why Social Media is Not Smart for Middle School Kids." *Psychology Today.* Retrieved from https://www.psychologytoday.com/us/blog/mental-wealth/201703/why-social-media-is-not-smart-middle-school-kids

DoSomething.org. (2019, January 28). "11 Facts About Cyberbullying." *DoSomething.org.* Retrieved from https://www.dosomething.org/us/facts/11-facts-about-cyber-bullying

Securly Blog. (2018, October 4). *"The 10 Types of Cyberbullying."* Retrieved from https://blog.securly.com/2018/10/04/the-10-types-of-cyberbullying/

Pacer Center's National Bullying Prevention Center. (2017). *"Cyberbullying: What Parents Can Do to Protect Their Children."* Retrieved from https://www.pacer.org/publications/bullypdf/BP-23.pdf

United Kingdom Department of Education. (2014, November). *"Advice for parents and carers on cyberbullying."* Retrieved from https://assets.publishing.service.gov.uk/government/uploads/system/uploads/attachment_data/file/444865/Advice_for_parents_on_cyberbullying.pdf

Family Lives. (n.d.). "Effects of cyberbullying." Retrieved from https://www.bullying.co.uk/cyberbullying/effects-of-cyberbullying/

Hinduja, S. and Patchin, J.W. (2018). *"Standing up to Cyberbullying: Top Ten Tips for Teens."* Retrieved from https://cyberbullying.org/standing-up-to-cyberbullying-tips-for-teens.pdf

CHAPTER THIRTEEN: CHILDREN WITH UNIQUE NEEDS

National Institutes of Mental Health. (2018, April). *"Autism Spectrum Disorder (ASD)."* Retrieved from https://www.nimh.nih.gov/health/statistics/autism-spectrum-disorder-asd.shtml

Centers for Disease Control and Prevention. (2019, August 27). *"Data and Statistics about ADHD."* Retrieved from https://www.cdc.gov/ncbddd/adhd/data.html

WebMD. (2018, November 12). *"What Are the Types of Autism Spectrum Disorders?"* Retrieved from https://www.webmd.com/brain/autism/autism-spectrum-disorders

Dunckley, V.L., M.D. (2016, December 31). "Autism and Screen Time: Special Brains, Special Risks." *Psychology Today.* Retrieved from https://www.psychologytoday.com/us/blog/mental-wealth/201612/autism-and-screen-time-special-brains-special-risks

Notes

DoSomething.org. (n.d.). *"11 Facts About ADD/ADHD."* Retrieved from https://www.dosomething.org/us/facts/11-facts-about-adhd

Becker, R. (2018, July 17). "Symptoms of ADHD in teens linked to heavy screen time." *TheVerge.com.* Retrieved from https://www.theverge.com/2018/7/17/17581486/adhd-digital-media-technology-teens

Mayo Clinic. (2019, June 25). "Attention-deficit/hyperactivity disorder (ADHD) in children." Retrieved from https://www.mayoclinic.org/diseases-conditions/adhd/symptoms-causes/syc-20350889

Klein, R.G., PhD. (2011, February 1). "Thinning of the Cerebral Cortex During Development: A Dimension of ADHD." *American Journal of Psychiatry, 168, 111-113.*

Notbohm, E. (2005). *"Ten Things Every Child With Autism Wishes You Knew."* Retrieved from https://handsinautism.iupui.edu/pdf/tenthingschild.pdf

About the Authors

DR. LISA STROHMAN is an attorney and licensed clinical psychologist who focuses her clinical practice on teens and families, providing a compassionate approach to traditional therapy. Her goal is to empower her clients to work with their own strengths to find solutions to get on the right path toward wellbeing. Dr. Strohman's most notable positions have been her work as a Legislative Assistant in Congress, an Honors Intern for the FBI, and a Visiting Scholar for the FBI while collaborating to complete her dissertation. After graduation she worked at a large law firm prior to completing her residency at the Arizona State Hospital with a clinical and forensic rotation in clinical psychology. Following residency, she learned to balance her clinical practice hours with her love of speaking by consulting with corporations, nonprofits, churches and educational partners across the United States. Dr. Strohman regularly appears on national news media as an expert contributor and is prolific in her writings on topics related to mental wellness and technology. She resides in Arizona with her husband and two children and continues her advocacy of technology wellness through the Digital Citizen Academy Foundation. **www.dcafoundation.org**

DR. MELISSA WESTENDORF is a licensed clinical and forensic psychologist in Wisconsin. Her education in law and psychology, coupled with her experiences, allow her to have a specialized understanding of the intersection of law and mental health. Her services include forensic psychological evaluations and outpatient therapy of adults and adolescents. Her goal in therapy is to help clients identify the thoughts, feelings, and behaviors associated with their life's struggles, while empowering them to continue making changes after therapy has concluded. In addition, she spends a great deal of time testifying in court as an expert in a variety of forensic evaluations. Dr. Westendorf presents on a variety of topics involving psycho-legal and ethical issues for psychologists and lawyers and has educated therapists around the United States and Canada on the legal and ethical responsibilities of providing telemental health services to patients and clients. Dr. Westendorf is a member of several state and national legal and psychological organizations and has served as a board member for many of those organizations. She also served as a board member of the Psychology Examining Board for the State of Wisconsin.

Made in the USA
Columbia, SC
28 February 2023

13093175R00135